365 FACTS YOU MUST KNOW

Om KIDZ | Om Books International

Reprinted in 2019

Corporate & Editorial Office
A-12, Sector 64, Noida 201 301
Uttar Pradesh, India
Phone: +91 120 477 4100
Email: editorial@ombooks.com
Website: www.ombooksinternational.com

Sales Office
107, Ansari Road, Darya Ganj
New Delhi 110 002, India
Phone: +91 11 4000 9000
Email: sales@ombooks.com
Website: www.ombooks.com

ISBN: 978-93-84225-33-9

Printed in India

10 9 8 7 6 5 4 3

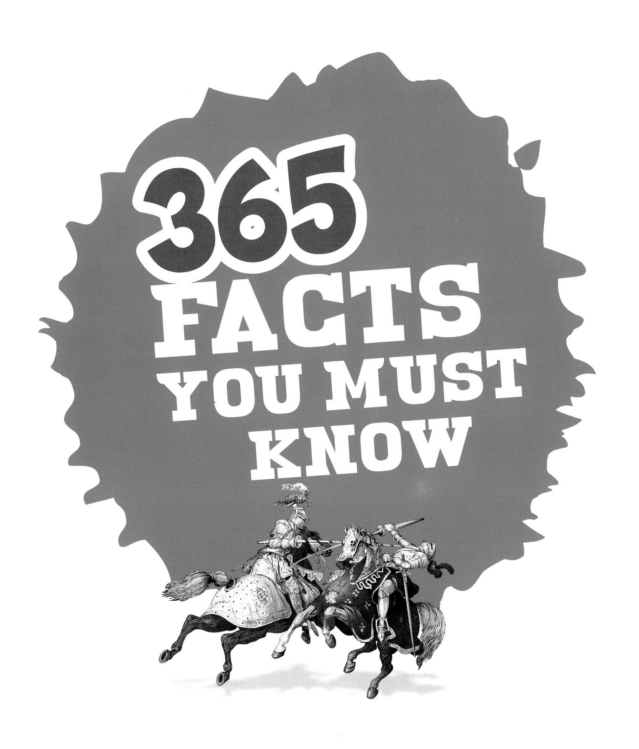

365 FACTS YOU MUST KNOW

An imprint of Om Books International

Contents

GET, SET, GO!

You have probably played games like football, basketball and cricket. You may even have modified them a little bit to suit the playground you were playing in. But were you aware that there are actual Quidditch tournaments that take place? Or that egg-throwing is a competitive sport? Or that boxing has been around for 4,000 years? Go on, read this section if you want to know more about these bizarre sports.

pg 70

ONCE UPON A TIME

Human beings started evolving more than 4 million years ago. But they started writing only 6,000 years ago. This means that we have no record of almost 90% of human history! However, we have been able to find out a lot about human life by piecing together the information we get from other sources like the tools that early humans used or from excavated cities. Find out more about some well-known and some not-so-well-known historical facts in this section.

pg 89

IN THE JUNGLE

pg 113

The natural world is a lot more interesting than you think. With more than 3,00,000 species of plants and close to 13,00,000 species of animals, some creatures are bizarre enough to put science fiction to shame! Take wild delight in discovering all you can about the different kinds of plants and animals that thrive on Earth.

YUM!

Food is the one thing that every human being has in common. Regardless of caste, creed and colour, every human being needs food to exist. Every country is known by its cuisine — we all know that Italy is the motherland of pizza and pasta, Arabia of meats and shawarma, France of baguettes and croissants and India of spicy curries. But we bet you didn't know that snails are a delicacy in France and that strawberries aren't actually berries at all! Read about more fantabulous food facts in this section.

pg 130

MONUMENTAL MARVELS

Since ancient times, man has created several magnificent monuments that have filled the world with awe. Whether these monuments have been created to honour a person or as a reminder of a significant event, they have gone down in history as marvels of architecture. Discover the story behind such marvellous monuments in this section.

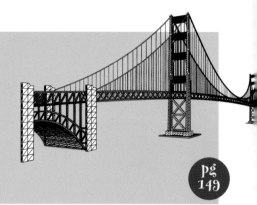

LITERATI

You've heard their names and you've read their books—well, some of them, at least. Authors, especially the great ones, have earned a reputation for being quirky and rather "odd" by normal standards. This means that there's a treasure of unknown facts about them and their works for us to explore! What are you waiting for? Flip to this section and learn all about these incredible authors.

ARTY PARTY

Art and art movements are an important part of our cultural history. Some artists, like Leonardo da Vinci, were also great scientists. Others pioneered art movements but were absolutely unknown in their day. Some others were celebrated artists even when they were amateur. Read this section to find out more about art and artists through the ages.

LIGHTS, CAMERA, ACTION!

The illusion of motion has left many spellbound and enraptured. Film has come a long way from the silent black-and-white films of the early 1900s. Though film is one of the newest forms of art, it has a fascinating story to tell. From the first film that had audiences screaming and running out of the theatre to the trivia about famous films, this section covers it all!

DOWN TO EARTH

Earth has been around for about 4.5 billion years now — that's 45 followed by eight zeros! Human beings, on the other hand, have been around for a measly 2 million years. In these 2 million years, even though we have discovered a lot about our planet, there is still a lot left to be discovered.

1 The speed of Earth's rotation is slowing down.

It's true that Earth is no longer spinning as fast as it used to. Around 200 million years ago, when dinosaurs roamed on Earth, a day was only 23 hours long. Today, Earth takes exactly 23 hours, 56 minutes and 4 seconds to complete a rotation. This means that Earth is slowing down at the rate of 1.4 milliseconds every 100 years.

This is due to the gravitational pull of the moon. The moon's gravitational pull causes a tidal bulge, which is a slight distortion in the shape of Earth during tides. This affects the speed of Earth's rotation.

2   Earth is not round.

As shocking as this sounds, it is true that Earth is
not perfectly round. It bulges at the equator and is
slightly flattened at the poles. The shape of Earth is
known as an oblate spheroid. This was first pointed
out by Sir Isaac Newton (of the "falling apple" fame).

The reason for this strange shape is the speed
at which Earth rotates. Have you ever seen a potter
mould a pot? A slight bulge appears in the centre
because of the spinning motion. The bulge on
Earth's surface is similar to this.

3   Earth enjoys its own private display of fireworks.

Also known as Aurora Borealis, the northern lights are a beautiful display of colourful
lights that can be seen in the night sky. However, this beautiful display can only be
enjoyed in the Northern Hemisphere or in very cold regions like Alaska and Canada.

Northern lights are created when charged particles, like electrons and protons,
from the Sun get trapped in Earth's atmosphere. When these charged particles come
in contact with gases like oxygen and nitrogen, they become electrically charged and
produce enough energy to create colourful lights.

4 There are at least eight lakes on Earth that are naturally pink in colour.

There actually are at least eight saltwater lakes on Earth that are pink in colour! Lake Retba in Senegal is one such lake that is nearly 40% salt. The Hutt Lagoon, Pink Lake, Lake Hillier and Quairading Pink Lake are lakes in Australia that are pink. However, the Pink Lake is not really pink throughout the year. When salinity rises in the lake water and the right amount of sunlight hits the lake, its algae turn into a mix of pink and red.

Salina de Torrevieja in Spain is another pink lake. Dusty Rose Lake in Canada is the only pink lake that is not saline and does not have any algae formation, yet is as pink as it gets throughout the year. Though there is no clear explanation for the colour, a common belief is that underground glacial water passes through rocks collecting minerals and sediments which give the water its pinkness. Masazirgol or Masazir Lake in Azerbaijan is the last of the "discovered" pink lakes.

These lakes are pink in colour because of a certain algae that breed only in saltwater.

5 The centre of Earth is a hot liquid.

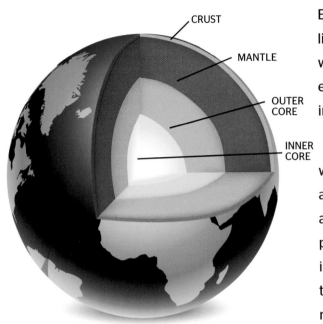

CRUST
MANTLE
OUTER CORE
INNER CORE

Earth is layered in spherical shells, much like an onion. Scientists believe that if you were to dig to the centre of Earth, you would encounter a huge ball of liquid and solid iron. This is known as Earth's core.

About 4.5 billion years ago, when Earth was formed, it was a hot ball of molten rock and metal. The heavier elements like iron and nickel sank down into the centre of the planet and formed the core. The inner core is solid, but the outer core is hot liquid. The temperatures in Earth's core are thought to rise up to 6,727°C.

6 Your weight differs depending on which part of the world you are in.

Gravity does not exert the same force uniformly across Earth's surface. This means that you would weigh more in some places on Earth than others. In fact, the same object is likely to weigh 0.5% more at the poles than at the equator. The reason for this is the slight equatorial bulge. Standing at the poles, you are likely to be significantly closer to the core of Earth than you would if you were standing at the equator, which affects the amount you weigh.

If you're on a weight-loss diet, it would be best if you steered clear of the poles!

7 The most expensive object ever constructed is the International Space Station.

The International Space Station is the biggest object to ever be flown into space. It travels around Earth at an average speed of 27,700 km/h, completing 16 orbits per day. At night, it can easily be seen from Earth as it flies 320 km above us. Around 16 countries, including the USA, Russia, Japan and Canada, and many European State Agency (ESA) member states worked together to build it. The International Space Station cost a total of 150 billion dollars to build.

In 1984, Ronald Reagan, then President of the USA, announced his support to build a base in space where people could live and conduct research. He believed that this project would be successful only if all the countries of the world cooperated and participated in building it. The first component of the station was launched in 1998. The first expedition to start inhabiting it was in 2000. As of 2015, it has been continuously occupied since then.

The International Space Station is about 109 m long. This means that it's longer than a football field!

8 Earth doesn't take 24 hours to make a rotation.

We're all aware that Earth rotates around its own axis. This means that at any time, half of Earth is facing the Sun, while the other half is facing away. It is day on the side that is facing the Sun and night on the other side.

Since we say that there are 24 hours in a day, it would be natural to think that it takes Earth 24 hours to make one rotation. However, this is incorrect. Earth actually takes 23 hours, 56 minutes and 4 seconds to complete a rotation.

9 Earth doesn't actually take 365 days to complete one revolution around the Sun.

Earth actually takes 365.2564 days to go around the Sun. Our calendar doesn't take into account 1/4th of a day each year. But since it's impossible to have 1/4th of a day, our calendar compensates by giving us an extra day once every four years. That's why there's a 29th February every four years! All years that are divisible by four (like 2004, 2008, 2012, 2016) are leap years.

Originally, people had calculated that one revolution takes 360 days. This was the norm till Julius Caesar and his astronomer studied annual events and created the Julian calendar, which is the base for the Gregorian calendar that we use today.

10   Only 3% of water on Earth is fresh water.

Fresh water is defined as water that contains less than 1,000 mg of dissolved solids per litre. This means that seas do not have fresh water, as they contain high levels of dissolved salt. Fresh water is required by all human beings, plants and animals (except animals that live in the sea) for survival. It is found in rivers, lakes, wells and glaciers. But the problem is that of the 3%, only 0.91% is actually drinkable since the rest forms the frozen ice caps in the North and South Poles. This is why it's important not to waste water!

11   Earth is being stalked by an asteroid.

On 27th July, 2011, the National Aeronautics and Space Administration (NASA) announced that our planet is being accompanied by an asteroid as it goes around doing its rotating and revolving. This asteroid was named 2010TK7 because the mission to find out more about this rock began in October, 2010. But it doesn't look like this asteroid is going to crash into Earth any time soon. It is around 300 m wide and revolves around an empty space at a safe distance from Earth.

12 Earth is literally recycled.

Though we've started becoming ecologically conscious only recently, Earth has been regularly recycling itself since the beginning of time! The "rock cycle" describes how rocks on Earth are formed. The liquid centre of Earth (called magma) moves upwards, crystallises and hardens into rock. These are called "igneous" rocks. Because tectonic plates below Earth's surface keep moving, these tiny rocks are lifted towards the surface. Wind and water erosion causes bits of these rocks to get shaved off. These shavings get buried and pressure from above helps them form another kind of rock, called "sedimentary" rocks. As these rocks get buried deeper, heat from Earth's core "cooks" them into "metamorphic" rock. When this rock gets caught in a spot where one piece of crust is pushing against another, it may get transformed back into magma!

Sometimes, the cycle skips a couple of steps. Magma from Earth's core spews out from volcanoes in the form of lava before turning into rock.

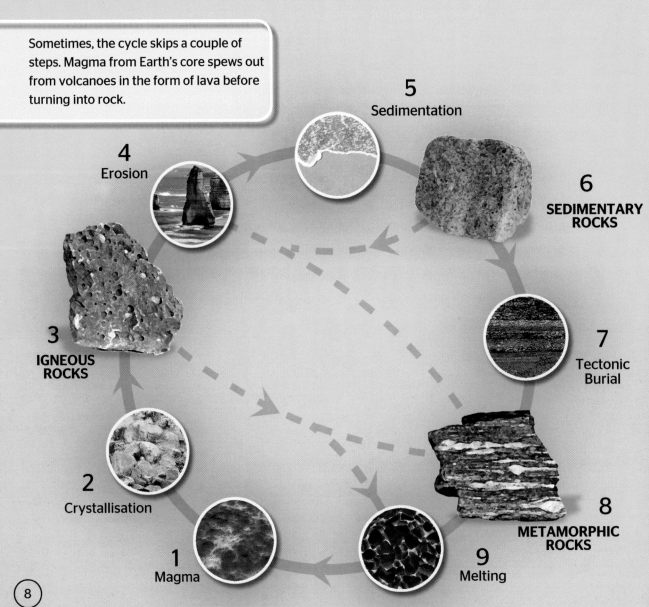

4 Erosion

5 Sedimentation

6 SEDIMENTARY ROCKS

3 IGNEOUS ROCKS

7 Tectonic Burial

2 Crystallisation

8 METAMORPHIC ROCKS

1 Magma

9 Melting

13 Earth is always spinning at around 1,600 km/h.

Even when you're standing absolutely still, you're never actually stationary. That's because Earth spins at a speed of around 1,600 km/h. So why aren't we all literally falling off the face of the earth? That's because we're all moving along with Earth at the same speed. It's exactly like why you don't fall off a speeding bus when you're sitting in the bus. But what's interesting is that not everyone on Earth is travelling the same distance—people on the equator travel much more than those at the poles. Think of Earth as a huge spinning basketball.

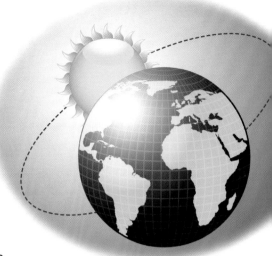

14 The highest point on Earth is not Mt. Everest.

Mt. Everest stands at an impressive 29,035 ft above sea level, which is quite tall. However, we already know that Earth is not perfectly round (remember the oblate spheroid?). So, anything along the equator is slightly closer to the sky. That's how Mt. Chimborazo in Ecuador beats the giant Everest. Though it is just 20,564 ft above sea level, it is located on the equator. Because of the extra bulge, it is technically further away from Earth's centre than Mt. Everest by around 8,000 ft!

15 Some caves are full of permanent icicles.

Natural formations called stalagmites and stalactites grow in certain caves that are made out of limestone. Stalagmites grow upwards from the ground and stalactites grow downwards from the roof. When water seeps into the limestone cave, it dissolves a substance called "calcite" found in limestone. When water moves through the cracks on the cave's ceiling, it drips onto the floor, leaving a little bit of calcite behind. As this keeps happening, the calcite builds up, forming a spiky structure hanging from the ceiling, called a stalactite. The water that drips onto the ground eventually evaporates, leaving behind slight traces of calcite which build up to form stalagmites.

16 The largest meteorite to fall on Earth made no crater.

The Hoba meteorite was accidentally found on a small farm in Namibia. Jacobus Hermanus Brits was ploughing his field when he heard a loud, metallic scratch and his plough came to an abrupt stop.

The obstruction was dug out and identified as a meteorite. It is the largest one to reach Earth intact. It weighs a whopping 60,000 kg and is 9 ft long, 9 ft wide, and 3 ft thick. This is why it has not been moved from its location. When the meteorite fell through Earth's atmosphere, it slowed down so much that it fell at terminal velocity, which is why it didn't form a crater.

17 The Death Valley is inhabited by mysterious ghost rock shifters.

The Death Valley is a hot and dry desert valley in California, USA. One of its most interesting spots is called "the Racetrack". Here, rocks weighing up to 320 kg mysteriously move across the desert, leaving long tracks behind. This brilliant phenomenon has even been captured on film! The stones move only once in two or three years, but the tracks formed last for three or four years. Though no one knows how these stones move without animal or human assistance, there are a few theories. One theory says that when the mud is damp and slippery, a strong gust of wind can set the rocks in motion. Then, even a wind that's not as strong can keep them moving. Another theory says that during winter, ice forms around the rock and on the ground, making the rocks slip.

In the 1840s, lots of people tried to cross the valley to reach the recently discovered gold mines on the other side. Due to the harsh conditions and a single death that occurred, people started referring to it as the "Death Valley".

18 There are some lakes on Earth that literally explode.

Three African lakes, Monoun, Nyos and Kivu, are rather hot-tempered lakes that are prone to exploding. This phenomenon was first observed on Lake Monoun in 1984, when it exploded and killed 37 people living nearby. The reason why these lakes behave so strangely is because they are located on a weak spot or a crack on Earth. Carbon dioxide, a gas, leaks out of these cracks into the lake. For some time, the leaked gas remains under the water, but sometimes, a tiny disturbance like a strong gust of wind or a slight landslide is enough to make the gas-filled water explode — somewhat like a bottle of champagne.

19 Earth is the only planet that is not named after a Greek or Roman god or goddess.

All the other planets in our solar system (Mercury, Venus, Mars, Jupiter, Saturn, Uranus and Neptune) are named after Greek or Roman gods and goddesses. The English language has borrowed from several languages. It evolved from Anglo-saxon (English-German), when a few Germanic tribes migrated to Britain in the 5th century. The Anglo-Saxon word "Erda" and the Germanic word "Erde" means land or soil. As the English language evolved, the word got transformed into "eorthe" or "ertha" till it finally became "Earth".

EORTHE
ERTHA
EARTH

20 The highest temperature recorded on Earth was 56.7°C.

The average temperature of Earth is around 14.6°C. The average temperature in the Sahara Desert, the hottest part of Earth, is 54.4°C. The hottest temperature ever was recorded at 56.77°C at Greenland Ranch in Death Valley, California, on 10th July, 1913.

The average temperature in Antarctica, the coldest part of Earth, is -51.1°C. The coldest temperature on Earth ever recorded was at -89.2°C in Vostok, Antarctica, in 1983.

21 There's a ring-shaped crater on Earth.

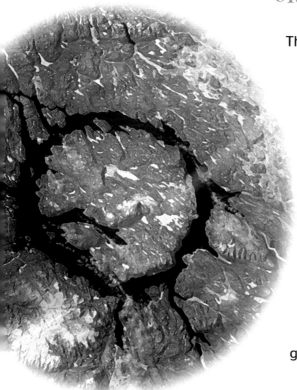

The Manicouagan crater in Quebec is shaped like a ring. Scientists estimate that the crater was created by an asteroid collision around 214 million years ago. While the outer area is depressed, the centre is raised in the form of a plateau, which makes the crater look like a ring when photographed from outer space. What probably happened was that the asteroid formed a round crater when it hit Earth. But the fluid pressure in this area was very high. This means that the water underneath kept pushing the land up. Slowly but steadily, the central part of this crater started rising. Water started filling the surrounding area, giving it a ring-like appearance.

22 Mt. Everest is actually growing every year.

It looks like enjoying the title of the tallest peak on Earth isn't enough for this mountain! This peak actually keeps growing by about 4 mm every year.

A long time ago, the Indian subcontinent was separated from the Eurasian continent by a large sea. But around 100 million years ago, India slowly began edging towards the larger continent at the rate of 4 inches per year. Back then, there were no mountain ranges bordering India on the north. It was only when India finally bumped into and collided with the rest of the landmass that the Himalayas were created. The tectonic plates under the continents kept colliding, giving rise to the Himalayan range.

Even today, this tectonic plate movement continues, making the Himalayas grow! Using the Global Positioning System (GPS), scientists have found that the Everest rises by about 4 mm every year!

On 29th May, 1953, Edmund Hillary and Tenzing Norgay were the first people to reach the summit of Mt. Everest.

23   The Mariana Trench is deeper than Mt. Everest put upside down.

Located in the Western Pacific Ocean, this trench is 25,42,000 m long, 69,000 m wide and 11,034 m deep. Mt. Everest, on the other hand, is only 8,848 m tall. The deepest point on the trench is the Challenger Deep.

But what's interesting is that though it is the deepest trench on Earth's surface, its bottom isn't the point of Earth that is closest to the core. This can also be blamed on Earth's shape. The trench is located near the equator. Since the equator bulges slightly (remember the oblate spheroid), it isn't the point closest to the core.

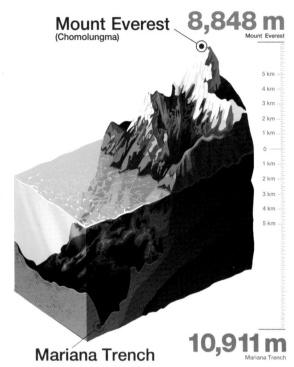

Mount Everest (Chomolungma) — **8,848 m** Mount Everest

Mariana Trench — **10,911 m** Mariana Trench

24   We have gold in our seas.

About 70% of Earth's surface is covered by seas. But we have only explored 5% of the underwater world! This means that 95% of the seas and marine life is still undiscovered! What's exciting is that there's about 18 million tonnes of gold dissolved in the sea and the rocks on the seafloor! But don't get too excited yet. The dissolved metal is so dilute that 1 litre of sea water contains only 13 billionth of a gram of gold. No one has yet discovered a way to extract this metal, but we can always keep our fingers crossed!

25 The Great Barrier Reef is actually living.

The Great Barrier Reef is the world's largest coral reef system. It is composed of roughly 3,000 individual reefs and 900 islands that stretch for 2,300 km over an area of approximately 3,44,400 km². The reef is located in the Coral Sea, off the coast of Queensland in northeast Australia.

The Great Barrier Reef can be seen from orbit and is the world's biggest single structure made by living organisms. This reef structure is composed of and built by billions of tiny organisms, known as coral polyps. The Great Barrier Reef supports a wide diversity of life and was selected as a World Heritage Site in 1981.

26 The North Atlantic Ocean is the saltiest ocean in the world.

How salty a sea or ocean is depends on how fast its water evaporates. When water from a sea or lake evaporates, it leaves salt behind. The North Atlantic Ocean water is the saltiest because of the currents that bring water into this part of the ocean. The Gulf Stream, which contributes to this ocean, originates in the very warm area of the Gulf of Mexico. This area has a very high rate of evaporation, which in turn leads to the increased saltiness in the North Atlantic Ocean.

27 The Sargasso Sea is a sea that doesn't border any land.

As strange as it sounds, the Sargasso Sea is not demarcated by land. It's demarcated by ocean currents instead! The sea is demarcated by the North Atlantic current in the north, the Canary current to its east and the North Atlantic Equatorial current in the south. The boundaries of the sea keep shifting since they aren't solid. How was this sea amidst the ocean spotted? Geologists spotted a vast patch of sea covered with free-floating seaweed called sargassum. They decided to name it the Sargasso Sea. This sea is home to many different species of marine life.

28 Earth might have once had a twin.

Though there is now no doubt that there's just one Earth, scientists estimate that 4.5 billion years ago, Earth may have had a twin planet called "Theia". It was roughly the size of Mars. They revolved around the Sun along the same orbit for millions of years till they collided. Earth absorbed Theia and the remaining debris helped form the moon. It is because of the additional mass given by Theia that Earth can sustain an atmosphere. However, this is just a theory and while many scientists believe it, an equal number of scientists also doubt it.

29 200 million years ago, all continents were actually one large landmass.

It has been proven that 200 million years ago, around the time when dinosaurs roamed on Earth, all land was actually part of one large landmass called "Pangaea". The northern part of this supercontinent was called Laurasia. It consisted of North America and Eurasia. The southern part, called Gondwana, consisted of Australia, South America, Africa, Antarctica and India. However, India later broke away from this large landmass and drifted towards Asia. When India collided with Asia, the tectonic plates underneath started pushing the land upwards and that's how the Himalayas were formed.

30 The Namib Desert is right next to the ocean.

The Namib Desert seems to be going through quite an identity crisis. It can't seem to decide if it's a desert or a beach! The wet winds that blow in from the ocean make the air humid. But since there are no hills or mountains to stop the winds and cause rainfall, the winds just blow past. Additionally, while blowing through the hot Namib Desert, most of their moisture evaporates, leaving the interior of the desert almost dry.

31 You can't actually sink in the Dead Sea.

The Dead Sea is a stretch of water around 80 km long and 18 km wide, with a salt saturation rate of 34.2%. This makes it 9.6 times saltier than the ocean. In fact, it's called the Dead Sea because no marine life can survive in such saline water. However, all that salt makes this sea denser than the human body, allowing you to float without any assistance! But be careful, because you can still drown. If you try to lie on your stomach, the density makes it impossible to turn back over. Accidentally drinking a few sips of the water is also dangerous since the human body isn't built to take in so much salt.

32 Angel Falls is the highest waterfall in the world.

Angel falls in Venezuela is 979 m high and is the world's highest waterfall. The waterfall drops over the edge of Mt. Auyantepui, down to the Kerep River, which is almost a kilometre below. The waterfall gets its curious name from Jimmie Angel, who was the first pilot to fly over these falls. The Canaima National Park, where this waterfall is found, has been declared as a UNESCO World Heritage site since 1994. It's quite difficult to reach the falls, which can only be accessed during the monsoon when there is enough water to take the boats up the river.

BODY OF KNOWLEDGE

The human body is unbelievably complex. It is so complex that even scientists haven't figured out everything about it yet. A healthy human body is, in fact, made up of millions and millions of tiny cells and other structures, each having a different job, working together like a well-oiled machine. Of course, we know that human beings have five senses and 206 bones. But there are a lot of interesting things about the human body that we bet you don't know!

33 The acid in our stomach is strong enough to dissolve zinc.

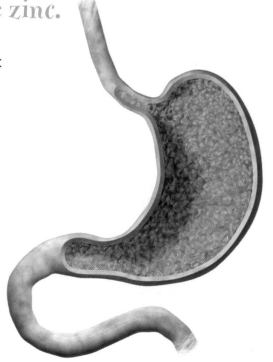

Woah! That's some strong acid! How is it that our stomach isn't constantly being dissolved by the acid that it produces? That is because our stomach walls generate cells so quickly that by the time one layer gets dissolved, another layer is ready to take its place. We also have a lining of mucous to help protect the walls of our stomach from the harmful effects of the acid.

We need the acid to help break down our food so that digestion is easier.

34 Nerve impulses to and from the brain travel at the speed of 273 km/h.

Have you ever wondered how you react to things so quickly or why you feel pain almost immediately when you prick your finger? It's because of the immense speed at which nerve impulses travel.

A nerve impulse is actually an electric charge that travels through the human body via structures called "neurons". This electric charge is caused by chemical changes in the neuron. Neurons are placed very close to each other with tiny gaps between them called "synapses". Neurons are generally negatively-charged in comparison to synapses. A neuron becomes activated when it senses that it is positive when compared with the outside. It quickly shoots a message through its body, which causes the next neuron to pick the signal up and so on — almost like a relay race.

When you prick your finger, the neurons near your finger send an electrical message to the next neuron, which in turn passes the information till the message reaches the brain. The brain then similarly sends a signal to the finger to move away from the source of pain. All this happens in the split second it takes you to jerk your finger away from the needle!

Some reactions are called "reflex actions". They don't need to travel all the way to the brain. They just travel to the spinal cord.

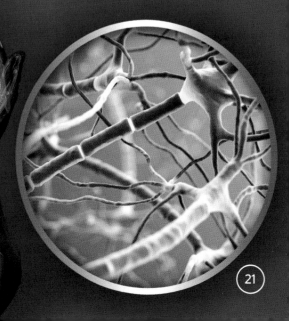

35 The human brain can hold up to 1,000 terabytes of information.

Scientists have yet to settle on the exact amount of information that a human brain can hold. Some estimates claim that if we were to convert our brain into a hard drive, it would probably be able to store 1,000 terabytes (TB) of information. The National Archives of Britain, which has documented about 900 years of history, only takes up 70 TB. Imagine how simple studying for exams would be if you could just figure out how to use all that memory space! A 128 GB iPod isn't looking so impressive now, is it?

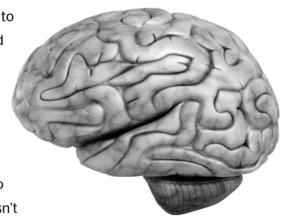

36 About 80% of the human brain is made up of water.

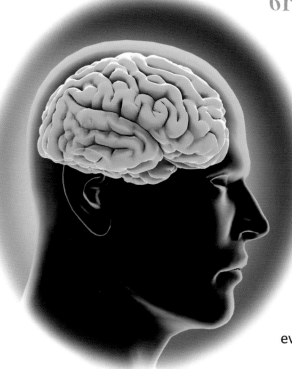

The brain is made up of special cells called nerve cells. And it isn't the firm, grey mass that is often shown in pictures. The live brain is a squishy, pink, jelly-like organ because of its high water content. The average adult human brain weighs approximately 1.3 kg. There are three parts in the human brain and each functions differently. The three parts are called the "cerebellum", "cerebrum" and "brain stem" (medula). The brain is the most important organ because it controls nearly everything the body does.

37 A single human hair can support almost 100 gm.

A single hair can roughly support the weight of two chocolate bars, which together weigh 100 gm! Each person has hundreds of thousands of hair on their head. Scientists estimate that if we were able to harness this strength, each head of hair would be able to lift 12 tonnes, which is as heavy as two elephants combined!

Another interesting fact is the rate at which hair grows. Each strand grows roughly a centimetre per month. This means that everyone grows approximately 16 km of hair per year!

38 The brain is more active when you are asleep than when you are awake.

Considering how much more active you are when you're awake, you would presume that the brain is also more active when you're awake. But this isn't the case. There are periods of time when you are fast asleep, but your brain is even more active than when you are awake! Scientists don't know why this is the case, but there's definitely a connection between brain activity and dreaming. The brain is more active during vivid, realistic dreams.

39 Fingernails grow three times faster than toenails.

Have you noticed that you need to cut your fingernails a lot more often than your toenails? If you thought that was strange, don't worry. Everyone's fingernails grow three times faster than their toenails. There are two reasons for this disparity. First, since fingers are physically closer to the heart, they get a better blood supply and flow of oxygen, stimulating their growth. Second, fingers are also busier than toes. Since the nails' main function is protection, the more "used" fingernails grow faster. On an average, nails grow about 1/10th of an inch each month.

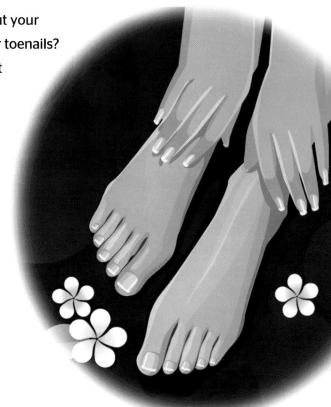

40 Human hair is almost impossible to destroy.

Hair is like the "Superman" of the body! Apart from burning it, there are very few things that can actually destroy it. Hair decays extremely slowly. It sticks around much longer than most other parts of the body. In fact, it decays so slowly that some Egyptian mummies dating back to thousands of years still have hair on their heads! Climate change, humidity and temperature changes leave hair intact, as do a variety of acids and chemicals. The only real weakness that hair has is fire, probably because it is made up of so much carbon (50%).

41 The surface area of a human lung is equal to a tennis court.

We know that we need to breathe in order to live. Our organs and cells need oxygen (found in fresh air) to live. They also need to get rid of all the carbon dioxide they produce while doing their jobs. Here's what happens to air when we breathe. From our nose, it goes into our wind pipe (trachea). The trachea branches into two (called bronchus), one for each lung. The trachea then further branches out into small twig-like structures called bronchioles. At the end of the bronchioles are small, sack-like structures called alveoli. They are surrounded by tiny blood vessels called capillaries. These capillaries absorb the oxygen from the alveoli and take them to the heart through red blood cells.

As each red blood cell deposits the oxygen it is carrying, it picks up carbon dioxide from the cells and heads back to the lungs. The alveoli again absorb this to be breathed out. All these structures in the lung increase its surface area, which is why the whole process happens so quickly—between the time we breathe in and out again!

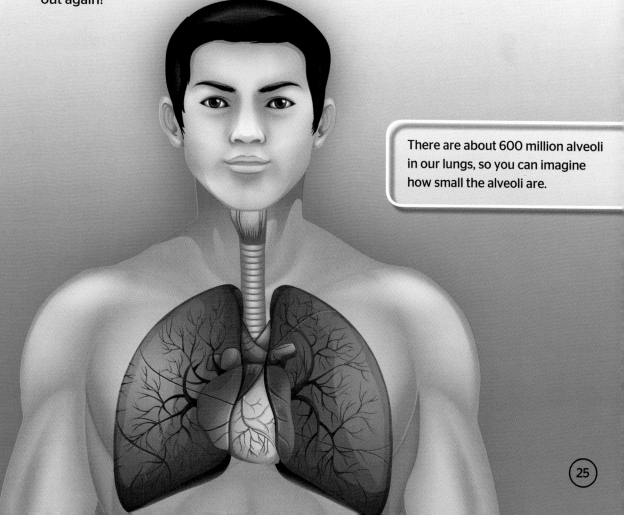

There are about 600 million alveoli in our lungs, so you can imagine how small the alveoli are.

42 You sneeze at the speed of 161 km/h.

Though individual speeds of sneezing differ, an average sneeze travels at 161 km/h. A sneeze starts in our nervous system. It actually helps keep the body safe by forcing bacteria and viruses out of the body. When the nerves in the nose sense a presence of something that isn't supposed to be there, they send signals to the brain to initiate a sneeze. Signals are rapidly sent to tightly close our throat, eyes and mouth. Next, our chest muscles vigorously contract and then our throat muscles quickly relax.

As a result, air—along with saliva and mucus—is forced out of our mouth and nose. Voila, it's a sneeze!

43 An average person produces enough saliva to fill two swimming pools through his/her life.

No matter how much we swallow it, saliva has this nasty habit of always being there. But do we really produce enough saliva to fill two swimming pools? Yes, we produce 1.5 l of saliva daily. What purpose does saliva serve, you might think? It actually lubricates the food we eat, which makes it easier to swallow. It also kick starts the digestion process by breaking down starch in the mouth itself. And believe it or not, it also helps us taste. We can only taste food that can be dissolved by saliva. Try wiping your tongue dry and then tasting something. You probably won't be able to taste it.

44 Your nose can remember 50,000 different smells.

When we smell something, it is because molecules from that object are travelling directly into our nose. There is a patch of neurons at the top of the nasal passages that end in hair-like structures called "cilia". When the smelly molecules reach these cilia, they trigger the neuron to perceive a particular smell.

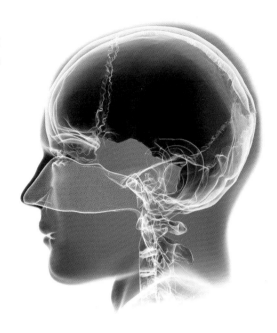

These neurons can distinguish between 50,000 different kinds of smells. Our memories are often connected to certain smells. That's why, sometimes, just a whiff of someone's perfume is enough to remind us of a person.

45 Babies are born with 300 bones, but adults have only 206.

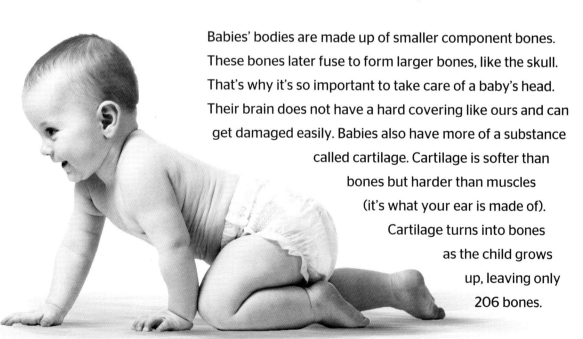

Babies' bodies are made up of smaller component bones. These bones later fuse to form larger bones, like the skull. That's why it's so important to take care of a baby's head. Their brain does not have a hard covering like ours and can get damaged easily. Babies also have more of a substance called cartilage. Cartilage is softer than bones but harder than muscles (it's what your ear is made of). Cartilage turns into bones as the child grows up, leaving only 206 bones.

46 The heart is the hardest working muscle in the human body.

Every time the heart beats, it is pumping out about 71 gm of blood. In a day, the heart pumps at least 6,000-7,500 l of blood.
The heart is constantly beating every second of the day — it doesn't even stop when we sleep! The heart has the ability to beat more than 3 billion times in one lifetime. This means that it has pumped 212 million l of blood in a lifetime.

Every day, the heart creates enough energy to drive a truck for 30 km. In an average human lifetime, that is equivalent to driving to the moon and back.

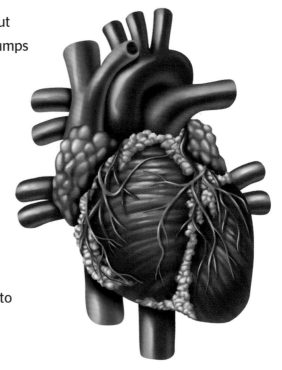

47 Human feet have 5,00,000 sweat glands.

We sweat because we need to regulate our body temperature. This means that we need to make sure our temperature is normal. Without sweat, our body wouldn't be able to tolerate all the heat it produces. That is why we sweat when we're nervous or worked up—our nerves get overworked, creating heat and causing us to sweat. We have 5,00,000 sweat glands on our feet, which can produce a pint of sweat in a day! Now you know why the feet are one of the smelliest parts of the body!

SWEAT GLAND

48 The small intestine is up to 23 ft long.

The "small" intestine is a very misleading name because this portion of the intestine is anything but small! It's 23 ft long, which is approximately the height of four adults on top of each other. The small intestine is coiled up; otherwise. it wouldn't fit in the abdominal cavity.

When you eat food, it goes from your mouth to your stomach through a long tube called the "oesophagus". Digestion begins in the mouth itself. Saliva breaks down certain food molecules in the mouth. The food then moves into the stomach, where the strong acid digests the food further. From the stomach, food enters the long roller coaster ride that is the small intestine. A substance called "bile" and other digestive enzymes help to break down the food. The food then moves to the large intestine, where water and some other chemicals are removed from it. Many bacteria in this part of the intestine also aid digestion. Finally, from the large intestine, the waste material moves and is stored in the rectum till it is excreted from the anus.

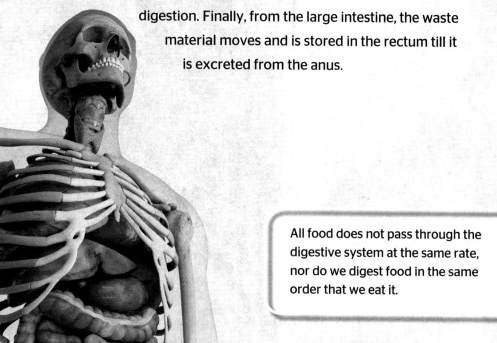

All food does not pass through the digestive system at the same rate, nor do we digest food in the same order that we eat it.

49 If you lay all your blood vessels in a line, they would go around the world twice.

Blood vessels are like tiny tubes in the body that carry blood from the heart to other organs and back to the heart. There are three types of blood vessels — arteries, veins and capillaries. Arteries carry fresh, oxygen-rich blood from your heart to the other organs and veins carry the deoxygenated blood back to the heart and lungs, where it gets oxygenated once again. Capillaries are thin vessels that carry blood to and from the fingertips and toes. If every vessel in the adult human body were to be attached and stretched, it would be so long that it could go around the globe twice!

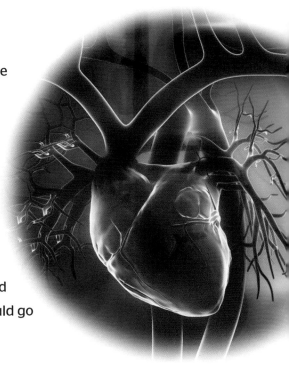

50 Humans shed about 6,00,000 skin particles per hour.

If you thought that only snakes shed their skin every once in a while, you were wrong! Humans also constantly shed their skin. No matter how much moisturiser you apply, you cannot stop your body from shedding skin. We shed about 600 g of skin each year. Don't worry, it's a good thing! It's just your body's way of protecting you from diseases and infections. Lots of fungi, bacteria, viruses and other nasty things find our skin very comfortable to live in. If we didn't keep shedding skin, we'd be a festering mess of a home to them!

51 Everyone has a unique scent.

Did you know that everyone smells? This doesn't mean that we stink, but we definitely have a particular scent that we can't wash away, regardless of how many times we bathe. This is because of certain chemicals that we secrete, called "pheromones". This is how dogs and other animals are able to follow a trail and sniff out a suspect by smelling his/her clothing or some other personal article. We don't use our sense of smell to recognise people because we can see and hear them. But people who are deaf and blind often rely on smell to distinguish between their friends.

52 The human eye continues to "see" an image even after it no longer exists.

The human eye retains an image on the retina for 1/16th of a second after it has disappeared. That's why characters on the television seem like they're moving! A film is actually nothing but a series of still photos that change at the speed of 16 per minute. Because the image of the previous image is still retained in the eye when the next image appears, the eye can "see" both of them, making it look like the image is moving. This is also why everything does not go black every time we blink—the eye "remembers" the image it was looking at.

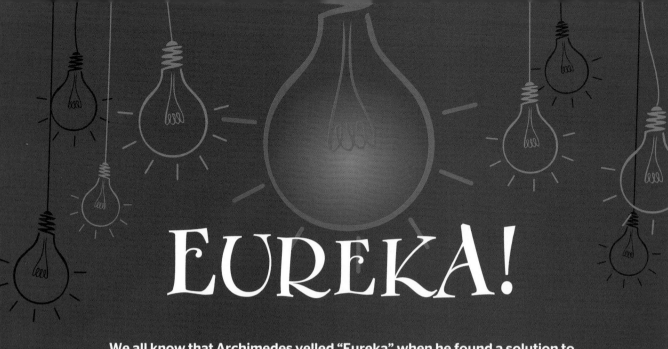

EUREKA!

We all know that Archimedes yelled "Eureka" when he found a solution to the nagging problem he had. But the stories of many other inventions have been lost along the way. Let's find out the story behind some of the products available in the market—some rather mundane, some quite necessary and others absolutely bizarre.

53 The microwave was invented by accident.

In 1946, a scientist named Percy Spencer was working for Raytheon Corporation. He was conducting radar-related research with a magnetron. A magnetron is a vacuum tube that releases microwaves to power radar equipment. Radar was vital for World War II. While working on the device, Percy noticed that the chocolate bar in his pocket started melting. He found this strange and started conducting more tests. Finally, by 1947, Raytheon Corporation had a 5-ft-tall, 340-kg microwave. By 1967, it had been refined to the countertop oven we're all so familiar with.

54 Doggy goggles are a multi-million dollar business.

Roni Di Lullo was just taking her dog for a walk one sunny afternoon when she noticed him squinting in the Sun. On an impulse, she tied her goggles to his head, creating the first pair of makeshift "doggles".

People soon started noticing her dog and asking for a pair for their own pooch. Roni set up a website, which was a huge hit. She could no longer keep up with the orders. So, she contacted eyewear manufacturers.

After quite a bit of research, this crazy product is finally available in stores and is actually in great demand!

55 There's a toy that is said to predict the future.

If the "Magic 8 Ball" has ever helped you to make a decision, you know what we're talking about. The Magic 8 Ball looks like a large snooker ball with a transparent window. The ball is filled with a dark liquid. A 20-sided die floats in the liquid. The die has a different outcome printed on each of its sides. If you ask the ball a question and turn it around to look at the transparent window, the die floats to the top to reveal the message.

56 The "X" in X-ray stands for "unknown".

German physicist Wilhelm Röntgen was experimenting with cathode ray tubes, which were somewhat like fluorescent light bulbs. He would suck all the air out of the glass tube, pump a special gas in it and run electricity through the gas. But something strange happened when the tube was surrounded by black cardboard. When he switched on his machine, a chemical that was a few feet away started to glow. The cathode ray tube was sending out invisible rays that could pass through paper, wood and even skin. The lit-up chemical in his lab was reacting to this. He named the phenomenon X-rays, where the "X" stood for unknown.

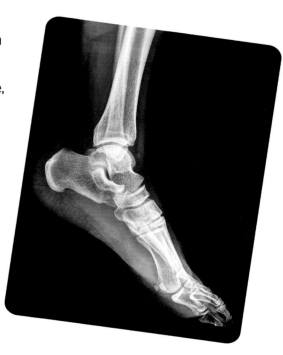

57 Matchsticks weren't common till 1826.

We're aware that man first discovered how to create fire by rubbing two flint stones together. You can imagine how inconvenient it must have been to rub two stones together till they sparked. The convenient matchsticks that we use today weren't invented till 1826. Jean Chancel, a French chemist, invented the first self-igniting match in 1805. However, it was extremely dangerous to use. John Walker invented the first modern matchstick in 1826, as he was stirring a pot of chemicals. He noticed that a dried lump had formed on the end of the mixing stick. He tried to scrape it off, when it suddenly caught fire. He first sold these "friction lights" at a local bookstore. They were 3 inches long and came in a box with sandpaper.

58 Stainless steel was the by-product of gun research.

For centuries, people have been creating steel by adding carbon to iron. Though steel had several advantages over iron, its major drawback was that it rusted easily. In 1912, an Englishman named Harry Brearly was trying to come up with a gun whose barrel would resist erosion.

Brearly failed several times. After many months, he noticed that all the steel scraps in his discarded pile were rusting, except for one that contained 13% chromium. He called his invention "rustless steel". It soon became popular for manufacturing vessels and cutlery.

59 Vulcanised rubber was the result of a fortunate mistake.

The problem with natural rubber is that it is not resistant to changes in the weather. It freezes and cracks during winter or melts into sticky goo in the summer. Charles Goodyear spent years trying to find a way to make rubber resistant to heat and cold. He finally succeeded when he accidentally spilled vials containing sulphur, lead and rubber onto a stove that was still warm. He noticed that in spite of the heat, the substance remained solid. That's how vulcanised rubber was born!

60 Flexible glass may have been invented around 20 CE.

Legend says that when ancient Rome was being ruled by Tiberius Caesar, a craftsman approached him with a bowl of drinking water. He claimed to have invented a technique by which he could produce "flexible glass". Caesar, not believing the story, threw the bowl on the ground, expecting it to shatter. To his surprise, it dented, but didn't shatter. The craftsman picked it up and fixed it with a small hammer. The Emperor asked him how many people knew about the method he used. The craftsman swore that he was the only one who knew. Caesar then ordered to have the man beheaded in order to stop the value of gold and silver from being undermined.

61 Robots were invented 240 years ago.

In the 1770s, Pierre Jaquet-Droz invented an incredible robot called "the writer". Called an "automaton", the robot looks like a boy. He holds a goose feather in his hand over a writing pad. One can feed text into the automaton by changing the letters on a wheel. Thanks to its complex mechanical clockwork, the automaton dips the quill in ink, shakes off the excess ink and proceeds to write. His eyes follow the quill as it is writing and his head tilts a little when he dips his quill in the ink. The automaton is still functional and is displayed at Musée d'Art et d'Histoire in Switzerland.

62 Post-it notes were an aeronautical experiment gone wrong.

In 1968, a chemist named Spencer Silver was working on inventing a strong adhesive for the aerospace industry for a company. But accidentally, he made the exact opposite — a weak adhesive. He noticed that his adhesive was unique because it was nearly indestructible. It would stick well even after several uses. He thought that it could be used to create a sticky surface for bulletin boards. He imagined people attaching notes to the board and peeling them off. Unfortunately, the idea didn't stick.

Several years later, another chemist suggested that instead of putting the adhesive on a bulletin board, it could be put on the paper. That way, the paper could stick to almost anything! With the help of a laboratory manager, they started manufacturing and marketing the little sticky notes. They handed out free samples and 90% of the people ordered more!

LET'S TALK

CHEER UP!

THANK YOU!

NO!

YES!

The standard Post-its are yellow because the manufacturers first used yellow scrap paper from the lab next door. When they ran out of scrap, they just bought more yellow paper.

63 Plastic was invented as a material used for insulation.

Leo Baekland, a Belgian-born chemist, was trying to create a replacement for shellac, a substance that was used as insulation in the early 1900s. Instead, he invented a combination of formaldehyde and phenol. He noticed that when he controlled the temperature and pressure, applied it to the two compounds and mixed the two with wood, flour, asbestos or slate dust, the substance was mouldable yet strong. It did not conduct heat and was thus heat-resistant. He called it "Bakelite". Over the years, Bakelite and its descendants (plexiglass, polyester, vinyl, nylon, etc.) have been used to make almost anything.

64 The idea of Velcro was inspired by a dog.

Georges de Mestral was hunting with his dogs in Switzerland when he noticed how many burrs had attached themselves to his pet. He also noticed how firmly they seemed to be stuck. He wondered what made them stick so firmly. He decided to examine them under a microscope. He noticed tiny hooks on the burr's body that caught on to his dog's fur. That is how the idea of Velcro was born. He experimented with many different materials, finally narrowing down to nylon. However, Velcro still wasn't widely used till NASA popularised it in the 1960s. Apollo astronauts used it to secure items that they didn't want escaping in their zero-gravity environment.

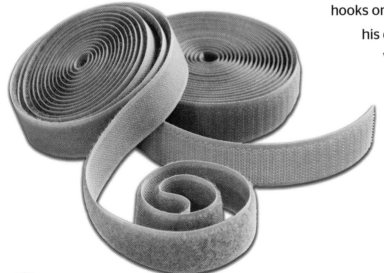

65 There's a doggy-translator available in the market.

There's a Japanese invention that claims to be able to interpret barks into human speech. This incredible product is called "Bow-Lingual".

Needless to say, it doesn't actually translate dog barks. It analyses the dog's emotion. Based on the tone of the bark, it deciphers what the dog is likely to feel and creates a phrase based on the sound of the bark. The Bow-Lingual then randomly selects a phrase that fits the mood and transmits it to the receiver. As exciting as this invention is, it's still to be seen how accurate it is.

66 Mauve dye was supposed to be an anti-malaria drug.

In 1856, William Perkin, an 18-year-old student, wanted to cure malaria. He was trying to create an artificial quinine, an anti-malaria drug derived from a tree bark. He was unsuccessful. However, he was curious to notice that one of his failed specimens was a thick, purple sludge. It was a unique shade of purple, a popular colour in the fashion world at that time. He was able to isolate the substance that was producing the colour and named it "mauve". Perkin never really cured malaria, but he created a storm in the fashion industry by inventing the first synthetic dye.

67 The design of the paperclip hasn't been changed since 1899.

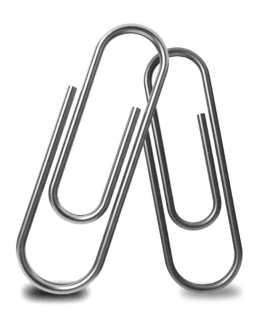

In 1867, Samuel B. Fay needed a way to attach tickets to garments without destroying the cloth. So, he bent a small piece of wire into a simple X shape. By sliding the ticket and fabric between the crossed wires, he could hold them together without damaging either. That was how the paperclip was born.

However, the pointed ends and limited strength were a major drawback. In 1899, William D. Middlebrook invented the paperclip as we know it today, along with the machine to produce it. And it has remained the same ever since!

68 The first computer mouse was made out of wood.

The computer mouse as we know it today was first developed by Douglas Englebart during the 60s. Back then, it looked like a large, rectangular block of wood with a button on top. Douglas was working at the Stanford Research Centre, a think tank sponsored by the Stanford University, while creating the mouse. He originally called it the "X-Y Position Indicator for a Display System". This mouse was first used with the Xerox Alto computer system in 1973. It wasn't very popular then and took some time to catch on. But today, it is nearly impossible to imagine a mouse-less computer!

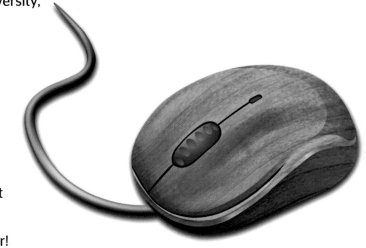

69 The zipper was invented 80 years before it actually became popular.

In 1851, Elias Howe patented "an automatic continuous clothing closure", very similar to what we now know as the zip. But it never reached the market. The design we use now is similar to the one patented by Swedish-born scientist Gideon Sundback. It was patented as the "hookless fastener". One of its first customers was the US army. It used zippers on the clothing and gear of its troops during World War I. The zipper only became popular after the B. F. Goodrich Company decided to market galoshes with Sundback's fasteners. They could be fastened with a single zip of the hand.

70 A spectacle-maker's son may have invented the telescope.

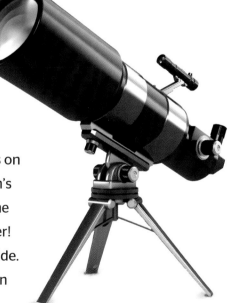

Most of what we know about space today is because of powerful telescopes. Legend says that the first telescope was discovered in the 1600s by a Dutch spectacle-maker named Hans Lippershey. One day, Hans observed his young son playing with two lenses on his workbench and holding them both at an arm's distance. When he looked through the lenses, the church across the road looked bigger and nearer! News of this great invention travelled far and wide. Eventually, it reached the ears of the great Italian scientist Galileo, who invented one of the most important telescopes in history.

71 Scientists are developing a laser that will tell us about the origin of the universe.

Extreme Light Infrastructure (ELI) is a new research organisation that aims to build the most powerful lasers in the world. They aim to build lasers that are 10 times more powerful than the best laser we have today. By 2017, they aim to combine 10 lasers to create a laser of 200 petawatts, i.e., in a fraction of a second, it shall produce 1,00,000 times more power than all the power stations of the world put together. The petawatt laser will have the power to break the vacuum of space. Scientists hope to finally crack the mystery of the origin of the universe with the help of this laser.

72 The invention of the world's first antibiotic was an accident.

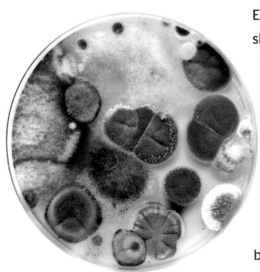

Every time you pop a pill to treat any disease, you should thank Dr Alexander Fleming and his accidental invention of penicillin in 1928. Dr Fleming was a famous researcher who often left his lab untidy. While experimenting with staphylococci bacteria, he went on a holiday with his family without covering the bacteria in the lab. On returning to his lab, he found that a green mould had accidentally fallen on the bacteria and killed it. He experimented with the mould and discovered that it killed many bacteria that infected humans. Dr Fleming called this first antibiotic "penicillin".

73 Superglue, when initially discovered, was rejected because it stuck to everything.

Harry Coover was trying to make clear plastic gun sights to be put on guns used during World War II. He didn't succeed, but he did end up making something far more useful — superglue! Harry stumbled upon a substance called "cyanoacrylates", but abandoned it because it was not suitable for his current project—it stuck to just about everything. Nine years later, he was working with Eastman Kodak, trying to develop a heat-resistant adhesive for jet canopies. It was then that Coover remembered his rejected cyanoacrylate, experimented with it, modified it and sold it!

74 There's a bulb that's powered by human blood.

We often go to great lengths to save electricity but designer Mike Thompson is way ahead of all of us. He invented a neon-blue bulb that is powered by human blood. Mike invented the bulb to spread awareness about the consumption of power and to make people realise that power is not an infinite source of energy. The bulb, called the Dracula Bulb, uses chemicals that are activated by human blood. The chemicals in the bulb mix with blood to release energy that makes the bulb glow.

75 There's a jacket that will make sure you are never lost.

We may have Global Positioning Systems (GPS) on our smart phones and tablets that help us find our way. But a Sydney-based company called Wearable Experiments has gone a step further. They have designed a jacket with an in-built GPS. The jacket has a custom-made mapping application, light-emitting diode (LED) lights and electric circuits that connect to a smart phone wirelessly. A person wearing the jacket can feed their destination on the phone and the jacket will guide them throughout the journey. The jacket lights up when the wearer approaches a turn. Known as the Navigation Jacket, it is designed by Billy Waterhouse.

76 Glow-in-the-dark roads may soon be a reality.

Street lights may soon become an obscure object from the past. A company called Pro-teq Surfacing has developed a spray-on paint that transforms regular roads to glow-in-the-dark roads at night. This substance, called Starpath, is water resistant. It absorbs the ultraviolet rays of the Sun during the day and releases this energy at night, making the surface glow. It can also be mixed with other materials, like stone, to make a non-slippery road, thus preventing accidents.

77 There are food wrappers that can be eaten.

Harvard Professor David Edwards found a unique way to reduce consumption and the wastage of plastic. He is the lead researcher of a French research team that

has developed edible food packaging to be used for liquids as well as solids. The edible food packaging is made of edible plastic, which in turn is made up of calcium and algae. Food particles are also mixed in the packaging to give a flavour of the food that is packed inside. The team has launched an ice cream called WikiCells with an edible outer coating and is experimenting on other products like fruit juices, chocolates and soups.

78 Inflatable seatbelts designed to provide extra protection may be the new rage.

People sitting in the front of a car are protected by air bags that inflate on impact. Scientists have now found a way to protect those seated in the back of the car too! Ford, an American car company, has invented a special seatbelt for the rear seat of its cars that automatically inflates to serve as an airbag during an accident. These seatbelts give extra care and protection to people in the rear seats, who are more vulnerable to head, neck and chest injuries. The seatbelts are currently found in Ford Explorer cars in the USA.

79 Steve Jobs visited India in search of "nirvana".

Steve Jobs started Apple Inc., a company that is known for its sleek designs and brilliant software. He is said to be one of the most brilliant entrepreneurs ever. However, Jobs wasn't always coming up with brilliant products. There was a time during the 1970s when he visited India to learn about Buddhism and search for enlightenment or "nirvana". However, his visit was unsatisfactory and he returned to the USA, eventually starting Apple and becoming a forerunner in the field of technology and innovation.

80 Sir Isaac Newton was a priest in the Church of England.

Sir Isaac Newton is well known for discovering gravity and his famous laws of motion. Though Newton was a scientist and had some rather unorthodox views about the Church, he was ordained as a priest since all Cambridge fellows were required to do so. It is said that he was sitting in a garden when he came up with his theory of gravity at the age of just 23! An apple fell on his head, prompting him to wonder why it fell down and not in any other direction. That's how he discovered that there is probably a force that keeps us all firmly rooted on the ground.

81 Albert Einstein was thought to be mentally retarded as a child.

Albert Einstein was born on 14th March, 1879. He was born with a disproportionately large head. In fact, his head was so big when compared with his body that the doctors thought he might be mentally retarded. Even as a child, he started speaking very late — it wasn't until his ninth birthday that he could speak clearly. It has been noted that a lot of brilliant people developed speech relatively late in life. This came to be known as the "Einstein Syndrome".

Einstein was a good student in school, though he didn't approve of the rigid methods of instruction. He graduated from school two years earlier than usual and wanted to enroll in the Swiss Federal Polytechnical School (Eidgenössische Technische Hochschule or ETH) in Switzerland. He failed his first attempt at the entrance test, though he tried again the next year and was admitted.

The pathologist who conducted Einstein's autopsy stole a part of his brain and kept it in a jar for 20 years.

82 Benjamin Franklin didn't "discover" electricity.

Benjamin Franklin is known for his famous kite-flying experiment. It is said that he attached a key to a kite and flew it during a thunderstorm in which he expected lightning. He connected the key to a leyden jar (a jar used to store electricity) by a thin metal wire. He then flew the kite with a silk ribbon, to prevent himself from getting the shock. When a thundercloud passed over the key, electric charge collected in the jar. Hence, Benjamin Franklin only proved that lightning is a form of natural electricity; he didn't actually discover it!

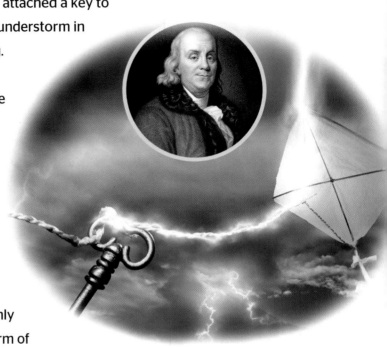

83 The pulley was invented in 287 BCE.

Archimedes is known for finding out how to measure the density of solids while he was bathing. He then ran down the street naked, yelling, "Eureka!" (which means, 'I have found it'). But he is also credited with inventing the pulley system, which is used even today, 2,300 years later! A pulley is a simple arrangement of wheels and ropes such that large weights can be lifted or moved using minimum force. In fact, Archimedes was so confident about his invention that he said, "Give me a place to stand and rest my lever on, and I can move Earth."

SPACED-OUT!

We're sure you know that Earth is just one among eight planets in the solar system. But did you know that our solar system is just one among more than 500 in our galaxy (the Milky Way)? And that the Milky Way is just one galaxy among possibly 100 billion galaxies in the universe? You can imagine how huge the universe might actually be. It's so large and complex, even our most powerful telescopes and smartest scientists haven't been able to find out everything about it.

84 Though Venus is farther away from the Sun than Mercury, it is hotter.

You'd think that the closer a planet is to the Sun, the hotter it would be. But though Venus is farther from the Sun than Mercury, it's much hotter. This is because of the atmosphere—or its absence. Mercury has no atmosphere.

Though it can be as hot as 426°C during the day, the temperature dips to -173°C at night. Venus, on the other hand, is 462°C during the day and remains constant even at night. This is because the atmosphere around Venus is made up of carbon dioxide, which traps a lot of heat.

85 Jupiter actually protects us from asteroids.

As the largest planet in our solar system, Jupiter seems to feel responsible for the well-being of the rest of the planets. Jupiter's radius is 69,911 km. Earth's radius, in contrast, is only 6,371 km. This means that it also has a lot of gravity. This gravity pulls in a lot of asteroids and debris that are floating around and would otherwise come hurtling straight at us. This was first observed by a Frenchman named Pierre Simon.

86 A season on Uranus lasts for 21 years.

Though a day on Uranus is just 17 hours and 14 minutes, a season goes on for years together. This is because Uranus' axis is quite tilted. It's tilted by 98°, which means that it's actually toppled on one side. This means that the Sun shines directly over one side of the planet, leaving the opposite side in darkness.

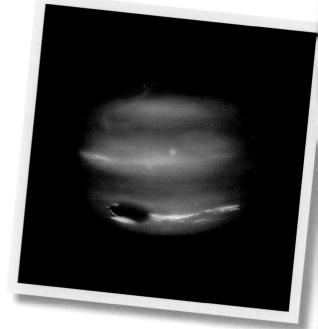

Scientists believe that this happened because a huge heavenly body, perhaps as large as Earth, hit Uranus when the solar system was first forming, which is why it is still rotating and revolving in the same position.

87 Pluto was named by an 11-year-old girl.

In 1905, an American astronomer named Percival Lowell noticed that the gravitational pull of "something" was disturbing the orbits of Neptune and Uranus. Unfortunately, due to the lack of technology in those days, he couldn't find out anything else about the mysterious "something". So, he decided to call it Planet X.

Around 25 years later, in 1916, 23-year-old Clyde W. Tombaugh from the Lowell Observatory finally managed to reveal the identity of Planet X.
On 13th March, 1930, Planet X's discovery was announced to the public. Suggestions for its name were also thrown open to the public. Finally, it was an 11-year-old from Oxford, England, Venetia Burney, whose suggestion was used. She suggested "Pluto". It was accepted because of the similarities between characteristics of the planet and the Greek God, Pluto (God of the Underworld). Also, the initials of Percival Lowell (PL) made up the first two letters of Pluto.

Pluto was considered a planet till 2006, after which it has been called a "dwarf planet" because the term "planet" was redefined.

88 Pluto isn't the only dwarf planet.

We now know that Pluto was stripped of its prestigious status as a planet and labelled "dwarf planet". But there are four other dwarf planets in our solar system too!

In 2006, the International Astronomical Union coined the term "dwarf planet". A dwarf planet is a celestial body that orbits the Sun. It is large enough for its shape to be controlled by its own gravitational pull. But it is not large enough for its gravity to pull in all the asteroids and debris in its orbit. Once Pluto was slotted into this category, scientists started relooking at other existing heavenly bodies to see if any of them fit into this category. Ceres was an asteroid that had been spotted in 1801. Initially, like Pluto, it had been considered a planet, till it was categorised as an asteroid and finally, a dwarf planet. Eris, Makemake and Haumea are the other dwarf planets.

Makemake made it into the list of dwarf planets in 2008, followed by Haumea in the same year.

89 The Sun isn't burning.

Contrary to everything you've heard so far, the Sun isn't a huge ball of fire up in the sky. It is actually a star. It's actually illogical for the Sun to burn, because everything needs oxygen to burn and there's no oxygen in space. The Sun's "glow" comes from the nuclear fusion. Nuclear fusion is a process by which two very tiny particles in the Sun, called protons, collide with such force that they get stuck or fuse. This creates huge amounts of heat and energy.

90 There are lakes on Saturn's moon.

Even though Earth is the only planet with water, it isn't the only planet with lakes. Saturn's moon, Titan, also has many lakes. But they are not filled with water. They are filled with liquid hydrocarbons like methane and ethane. Their highly-toxic atmosphere is made of nitrogen and methane. They are completely still during winter. But scientists expect the climate to warm up by 2017, when strong winds will cause waves in these lakes.

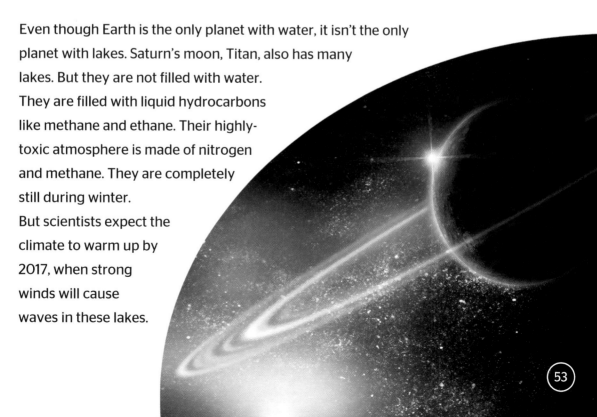

91 It rains on other planets too.

We know that it is nearly impossible for water to exist on any planet other than Earth. But scientists have observed rain on other planets too! Obviously, it isn't water that pours down on these planets. As many toxins like ethane, methane and sulphuric acid make up the atmosphere of other planets, the liquid form of these toxins rains down on these planets. To add to the misery of these planets, they also face storms and hurricanes that are a hundred times more violent than the ones we witness here on Earth.

One such example is the Great Red Spot on Jupiter. This is a hurricane that seems to have lasted for 500 years now! This eternal storm was discovered by Galileo when he first pointed his rudimentary telescope at Jupiter in the 1600s!

Venus is considered to be very similar to Earth, except that it has sulphuric acid instead of water. In fact, when this acid rains down, it evaporates before it touches the ground.

92 There are "solar storms" every 11 years.

A solar storm is a large wave of magnetic particles that the Sun sometimes sends into the solar system. There are certain spots on the Sun's surface that appear as dark spots when viewed through a telescope. These are cold regions on the surface of the Sun. Every 11 years, these cold regions cause a solar storm. There is a slow build-up of magnetic energy on the Sun's surface. This build-up continues until the Sun can't take it anymore and the cloud explodes, sending magnetic waves our way!

93 When you look at the sky, you are literally looking back in time.

The stars we see in the sky are actually very far from us. Light takes a very long time to travel from the star to our eyes. This means that every time we look at a star "twinkling", we're actually seeing what they "looked" like in the past. For example, Vega is a star that is just 25 light years away from us. This means that light from this star takes 25 years to travel to Earth. So, when we look at it, we're actually seeing it from 25 years ago!

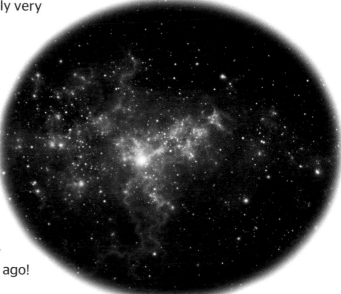

94 The Hubble telescope lets us look billions of years into the past.

We can see objects that are very far from us through the Hubble telescope. Thanks to this telescope, NASA has been able to create some incredible images, one of which is the Hubble Ultra Deep Field.

This picture shows us a tiny patch of the night sky in immense detail. It contains 10,000 objects, most of them being young galaxies. This picture acts as a portal back in time. It transports us 13 billion years into the past, just 400 to 800 million years after the Big Bang, which is actually very early in terms of the universe's history.

95 There's a diamond in space that's named after a Beatle's song.

Scientists have found the largest-known diamond in the universe 50 light years away from Earth. In the constellation of Centaurus, there is a diamond that has a diameter of 4,000 km! It weighs in at a massive 10 billion trillion trillion carats. That's one HUGE diamond, isn't it? Though its official name is BPM 37093, it is also called "Lucy" after the Beatles' song, "Lucy in the Sky with Diamonds".

96 Black holes are large stars running out of fuel.

Black holes are large, black splotches in space. One can't actually "see" a black hole because it's so black, but its presence can be confirmed by the behaviour of objects surrounding it. Stars are made up of gases like hydrogen and nitrogen that serve as fuel. At some point in time, this fuel runs out. Once this happens, the star starts shrinking because it isn't creating energy any more. It grows smaller and smaller until it becomes as small as an atom.

As a star that was originally so massive is now barely the size of an atom, its gravitational pull grows tremendously. The star begins collapsing into itself. While doing this, it begins attracting everything that's around it, including light. That's why black holes seem so black. Even light cannot escape their gravitational pull.

The nearest black hole is 1,600 light years away. That is about 15 quadrillion km for Earth.

97 Our Sun takes 225 million years to travel around the galaxy.

Just like the moon revolves around Earth, and Earth and all the other planets revolve around the Sun, the Sun itself orbits around the centre of our galaxy, the Milky Way. This means that our entire solar system itself is constantly revolving around the centre of our galaxy. It takes the Sun about 225 million years to complete one whole circuit of the galaxy. The last time the Sun was in its current position, the super-continent Pangaea was just breaking up and dinosaurs were first making an appearance!

98 The tallest mountain in our solar system is on Mars.

Olympus Mons on Mars is the tallest mountain in the solar system. This gigantic mountain is 26 km tall and 600 km wide. This means that it's almost thrice the height of Mount Everest. Volcanoes in Mars are so much taller than those on Earth because of the lack of plate movement beneath the planet's surface. This is why the volcanoes erupt more often and lava just keeps building up.

99 A year on Venus is shorter than its day.

All planets rotate on their own axes. The amount of time that a planet takes to complete one rotation is called a "day". At the same time, planets are also revolving around the Sun. The amount of time that a planet takes to complete one revolution is called a "year". Venus takes much longer to rotate on its axis than it does to revolve around the Sun. It takes a little less than 225 days to revolve around the Sun once, but 243 days to rotate on its own axis. Technically, this makes a day longer than a year on the planet.

Another interesting fact about Venus is that it rotates in a different direction as compared with the rest of the planets. All planets rotate counter-clockwise when seen from above the North Pole. Venus, however, turns clockwise.

Another thing that sets Venus apart from the rest of the planets is that its axis is not tilted at all. This means that no part of the planet is closer to the Sun, so the temperature is uniform on the entire planet throughout the year—at around 461° C.

100 The fastest known spinning objects in the universe are neutron stars.

A neutron star is created when a giant star dies in supernova. A supernova occurs when a huge gas star explodes. Gravity then causes all the protons and neutrons to fuse together, which is why the star if called a "neutron star".

It is so dense that if you were able to scoop out a single teaspoon of the star, it would weigh more than a hundred billion kg! The power from the supernova gives the star a very quick rotation. The fastest known neutron star spins 24% faster than the speed of light, which is 70,000 km per second!

101 There could be 500 million planets that are capable of supporting life in our galaxy.

It's quite coincidental that Earth has the perfect conditions to support life—its distance from the Sun ensures the perfect temperature, water can exist as a solid and a gas, and the atmosphere contains all gases required to support complex life forms. But our solar system is just one among at least 50 billion in our galaxy. If any one of these have conditions similar to Earth, they could support life. These planets are called "Goldilocks Planets" and scientists searching for extraterrestrial life on these planets.

102 Saturn is light enough to float on water.

If we could produce a vessel large enough, we would be able to see Saturn float on water. Though Saturn is 80 times larger than Earth, if both planets were to be dropped in the ocean, Earth would sink to the bottom, while Saturn would be bobbing up and down on the surface. This is because of the different densities of the planets. Saturn's density is 1/8th that of Earth and 2/3rd of water. Since Saturn is less dense than water, it would float.

Apart from this, though Saturn is the second largest planet in the solar system, its gravitational pull is almost the same as that of Earth. This means that this planet is quite light and fluffy. In fact, it's sometimes called the "gas giant". Saturn has no solid surface. Its surface is made up of gases. So, it's difficult to see where Saturn's atmosphere actually begins.

Saturn rotates at a very high speed. While one day on Earth is 24 hours, a day on Saturn is just 11 hours.

103 There are probably more than 170 billion galaxies in the observable universe.

The "observable universe" refers to the part of the universe that we can see from Earth with our current technology. There are different estimates for the number of galaxies within the observable universe, but data from the Hubble Telescopes estimates a whopping 170 billion galaxies! And that's just in the observable universe—there may be a lot more out there in space that our technology hasn't advanced enough to detect yet!

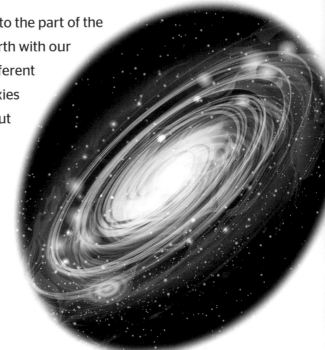

104 We are all made from stardust.

This may sound like something out of a fairytale, but it's true. Almost every element on Earth was created in the burning core of a star. Since we are made from elements found on Earth, this means that all animals, plants and even human beings are made from stardust. In fact, 90% of our body is stardust as all elements except hydrogen and helium are created in stars. Carl Sagan, a well-known American astronomer, says, "We are made of starstuff."

It is estimated that our Sun will become a Red Giant in 5 billion years and will destroy Earth in the process.

63

106 There's a planet that orbits a strobe-like star.

All planets revolve around a star. All the planets in our solar system revolve around the Sun. But there's a planet called PSR B1257 + 12 b which orbits a nuclear star. All nuclear stars spin incredibly fast. But some of them continue to spit out radiation and light even after their death. These stars are called "pulsars". This means that they look like huge disco balls in space. PSR B1257 + 12 b revolves around one such nuclear star! In fact, the planet gets so much radiation that one side of it actually glows!

107 There's a planet that is completely dark.

TrES-2b has been called the "dark planet" because it reflects no light. It looks just like a large, coal-black ball of gas floating around space. The planet has no atmosphere or clouds because its temperature is 1,000°C—too hot for clouds. Clouds may have helped the planet reflect some light. But TrES-2b reflects only 1% of light that falls on its surface, which makes it the darkest planet to be discovered. Scientists don't know why it is so dark, but they say that it may be because the planet's composition is like potassium or sodium, which absorbs light.

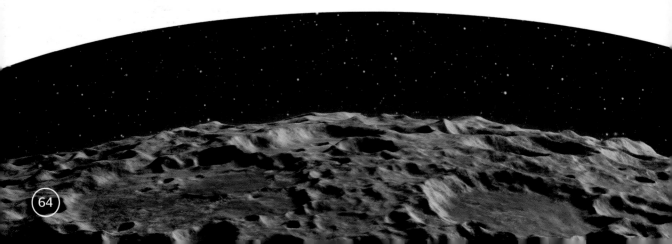

08 There's another planet that might be able to sustain life.

A few planets have been discovered that may be able to support human life. Of these planets, the one that's most likely to host life is called Gliese 581 c. But it looks completely different from Earth! The planet revolves around a red dwarf, so the sky always has a red tinge. This red light would affect all vegetation. Plants would need to modify themselves in such a way that they can perform photosynthesis even with this infrared light. This would mean that every plant on the planet would be pitch black!

This planet is so close to its star that it doesn't rotate any more. One side of the planet is constantly facing the star while the other side is constantly facing away from the star. The side facing the star is too hot and bright, while the other side is too dark and cold. The only place where any organism could survive is the narrow strip between the two where the temperature is just right.

In October 2008, we sent a message from Earth directly to Gliese 581 c. It is expected to reach the planet around 2029.

109 A supernova explosion caused Earth to be lit up for months.

The Crab Nebula was produced by a supernova explosion in 1054 CE. Chinese and Arab astronomers at the time noticed the explosion. It is said that the explosion was so bright, it was visible during the day and lit up the night sky for months later. It can still be seen with the help of the Hubble Space Telescope. At the centre of the nebula is a neutron star that rotates at a speed of about 30 times each second. The nebula is shaped (not surprisingly) like a crab.

110 Gravity can "bend" light.

We've already spoken about black holes and how their gravity is so great that even light gets sucked in. But gravity can also "bend" light, which means that what we see from Earth may not actually be where it seems to be. Scientists call this "gravitational lensing". This is actually advantageous for astronomers because it means that they can study things that are actually behind objects that exert a lot of gravity, like large galaxies, without actually going into space. The gravitational lens can sometimes make multiple copies of objects in the sky.

111 You can see 150 billion billion miles with your naked eye.

The Andromeda Galaxy, which is 150 billion billion miles away, is the furthest object that you can see with the naked eye. It is the closest galaxy to the Milky Way. It is about 2.5 million light years away. This means that when you look at the galaxy, you are looking at light which actually left the galaxy 2.5 million years ago! It contains about 1 trillion stars. Our galaxy, the Milky Way and the Andromeda Galaxy are expected to collide in 4.5 billion years.

112 There's a huge cloud of gas that's made up of a billion billion litres of alcohol.

Sagittarius B is a large cloud of gas that floats near the centre of the Milky Way. It is 26,000 light years away from Earth. It is around 463,000,000,000 km in diameter and made up entirely of alcohol! The presence of organic molecules (alcohol) suggests that life on other planets might be possible. The structure of this cloud is very complicated with varying densities and temperatures.

113 There are fossil fuels on Saturn's moon, Titan.

Saturn's moon, Titan, is the only moon we know of that has an atmosphere of its own. In 2005, a probe was sent to this moon, which revealed that even Saturn's rings were not visible from Titan because of its thick atmosphere and stormy weather—except that instead of water, it rains fuel!

This is because of croyovolcanoes, which are like volcanoes, except that they spew out water and ammonia instead of lava. The clouds are made of liquid methane, which is what natural gas on Earth is made of. In fact, there are rivers and oceans on Titan that are made of this gas-rain. Just the polar lakes on Titan contain hundreds of times more oil and natural gas than every known oil and gas reserve on Earth. If only we could find a way to ship all this fuel to Earth, our energy crisis would be solved!

Scientists suspect that there may be life forms on Titan that use methane instead of water for its primary functions.

114 The human brain is the most complex object discovered in the universe.

Nothing in the thousands of galaxies discovered so far compares to the human brain in terms of complexity. With a hundred billion neurons and a quadrillion connections, our brain is constantly busy. Our brain stores information on language, culture, consciousness, idea of self, ability to learn and even an inbuilt "model of gravity" that ensures we're constantly standing upright. Our brain is active even when we are asleep to control our bodily functions.

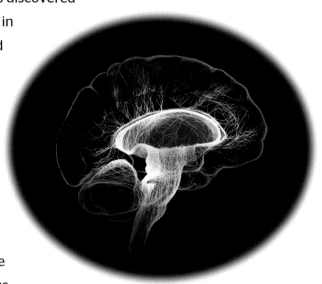

115 Scientists say that 275 million new stars are born every day.

Stars form out of collapsing clouds of dust and gas. As the cloud collapses, its temperature and density increases. The object that is formed at the centre of the cloud, which will become a new star, is called a "protostar". The protostar is surrounded by a cloud of gas and dust. Any light that the star emits is absorbed by this dust. Later, once the star is hot enough for its radiation to blow away all the material that is surrounding it, it becomes a star. That's how stars are formed. Scientists estimate that 275 million new stars are created on a daily basis.

GET, SET, GO!

You've probably played games like football, basketball and cricket. You may have even modified them a little to suit the playground you were playing on. But were you aware that there are actual Quidditch tournaments that take place? Or that egg-throwing is a competitive sport? Or that boxing has been around for 4,000 years? Go on, read the section if you want to know more about these bizarre sporty facts.

116 There's a sport that combines chess and boxing.

You have probably heard of sports that involve mental prowess and others that require physical strength. But have you heard of a hybrid sport that combines the two? Iepe Rubingh invented a sport named chess boxing that is exactly what it sounds like—a mixture of chess and boxing! Alternate rounds of chess and boxing of three minutes each take place in chess boxing. A person has to be skilled at boxing and chess to win this game, as either game can decide the winner.

117   People play hockey underwater.

In this sport, teams manoeuvre a puck with a foot-long stick at the bottom of a swimming pool in goals that are 9 ft apart. The teams have 10 players each, out of whom four act as substitutes. They are not in the water for more than 5-15 seconds at a time.

It is believed that underwater hockey was invented as early as 1954 by a man named Alan Blake and was initially called "Octopush". But the British Navy is claiming to have invented it to keep their divers fit and improve their efficiency in water. Southsea Sub-Aqua Club is believed to have invented it to entertain its members during the winter months.

118   Rock, Paper, Scissors is played at a professional level.

We have all played rock, paper, scissors as children. But who would have thought that this childhood game could transform into a worldwide championship? Rock, paper, scissors is a contest between two people. It involves the use of one's hands only. International competitions of rock, paper, scissors are held throughout the world.

Rock, paper, scissors is believed to have originated in 220 BCE in China when the Han dynasty ruled it. It was referred to as "shoushiling" or hand command.

119 There's a sport where the person with the weirder face wins.

Do you know that if you are good at making weird facial expressions and distorting your face, there might be a sportsperson in you that you are not even aware of? Gurning is a sport where the participants distort their faces. A panel of judges decides the winner of the competition. It is believed that gurning originated in England during the 13th century in the Egremont Crab Fair, which was given a Royal Charter by King Henry III. Participants sometimes use a horse collar around their neck as well. The World Gurning Championship is held in Egremont, Cumbria, in England every year.

120 Buzkashi is the national sport of Afghanistan.

Buzkashi in Persian means "goat dragging". As the name suggests, the game does include a goat that gets dragged. The game is played in many central Asian countries and is even the national sport of Afghanistan. The game involves the carcass of a goat or a calf, which the players (on horseback) fight to gain and keep control of. The carcass usually weighs anything between 20 and 50 kg. There are few rules in the game, though etiquette demands that players do not bite, pull hair or use any weapons while playing the game.

121 The first basketball net was a peach basket.

Dr James Naismith, a Canadian physician interested in sports physiology, taught at Springfield College in Massachusetts as a physical education teacher.

Dr Naismith wanted to start a new game to engage the school's football and rugby players during the winter months. He found a peach basket in a janitor's closet and hung it on a railing, 10 ft above the floor. The players shot the ball into the basket as a sport, but every time they did that, they had to get the basket down to take the ball. Dr. Naismith decided to cut a hole in the basket so the ball would come down on its own. The first 13 rules of basketball were written down on 21st December, 1891.

DR. JAMES NAISMITH   KANSAS

US servicemen popularised basketball during World War II in many countries throughout the world. The popularity of the game also increased in colleges throughout the USA, which paved the way for professional basketball. The National Basketball League was founded in 1898, which merged with the Basketball Association of America to create the National Basketball Association (NBA). The NBA not only conducts matches, but also protects players from abuse and encourages a less rough game.

122 Boxing has been a popular game for at least 4,000 years now.

Have you ever wondered how boxing originated as a sport? Paintings from the Egyptian Civilisation dating back to 2000 BCE depicting fist fights and spectators have been found. The origin of boxing is disputed. Initially, boxing consisted of just bare fist fighting between willing or unwilling participants. Ancient Greek history even says that this was a sport enjoyed by Greek Gods. Some believe that a person used his fist on another person in a play and that's how boxing was invented!

Boxing was popular during the Roman times. Players wore metal hand coverings and the games often ended with the death of one opponent. Boxing diminished for sometime after the fall of the Western Roman Empire. The game resurfaced in England in the 18th century as bare-knuckle fighting during the Industrial Revolution. The first championship was held in 1719 in London and for the first time, the term "boxing" was used.

123 Cheese rolling is a popular competition in England.

Most cheese lovers would be aghast to know that people voluntarily waste so much cheese. In this rather bizarre sport that's held in Gloucester, England, people roll a 9-pound block of cheese downhill and run after it. The person who reaches the finish line first is the winner. The winner is given the cheese as the prize! Since 2013, the cheese has been replaced by foam for safety reasons. Cheese rolling competitions grew popular and are now held in some parts of the USA as well.

124 "Skeleton" is a legitimate Winter Olympic sport.

As ominous as the name sounds, it does not come within an inch of how dangerous the sport actually is. This game is a fast, winter, sliding sport in which a person lies face down on a narrow sled and hurtles down a frozen slope at speeds that could reach over 130 km/h. The game is thought to have originated in 1882, when English soldiers constructed a toboggan track between two towns. It was introduced in the Olympics in 2002.

125 Live pigeon shooting was once an Olympic sport too.

Many shooting events were held in the 1900 Olympic Games; live pigeon shooting was one of them. The participants of this event had to kill as many live pigeons as they could. This was the first and only time in the history of Olympics that live animals were used and killed for sport. The pigeons were released from a trap and the participants shot them. Around 300 pigeons were killed during this event. It received a lot of criticism and its records were erased from the official Olympic records.

126 Official "shin kicking" exists too!

Shin kicking or hacking as it is popularly known is a sport in which two participants kick each other on the shin in order to throw the other on the ground.

Shin kicking is sometimes referred to as the English martial arts. It is believed to have originated in England in the early 17th century. Old stories and legends convey the use of steel-toed boots during the competition.

It is believed that the participants hit their shins with hammers to build tolerance towards pain.

127 Racing with beds is another strange British sport.

Bed racing as an event originated in the North Yorkshire town of Knaresborough, England. In this event, several teams of seven members take part. The event involves the creation of a bed based on a theme given by the organisers.

One participant must sit on the bed. The bed should have four wheels and it must float in water as well. The participants run with the bed across the route and cross a river too. The team that reaches the finishing line first wins the competition.

128 Oil wrestling is the national sport of Turkey.

The national sport of Turkey is oil wrestling. In this sport, two people wrestle after having lathered themselves with oil. Oil wrestling or "grease wrestling" as it is popularly called, is a sport in which the participants put olive oil on their bodies and wrestle each other. Wrestlers wear hand-stitched pants called kisbets

that are made of animal skin. Earlier, matches went on for one or two days till one participant could prove their superiority over the other. Now, the time limit is restricted to 40 minutes per match.

129 "Poohstick" championships are held annually.

Who would have thought that a simple game played by cartoon character Winnie the Pooh in a book could become an actual annual sporting event? World Poohsticks Championships are held at Day's Lock on River Thames in the UK every year. The participants throw a stick in the river. The participant whose stick reaches downstream first is the winner.

The bridge and the sport became so popular that the original bridge was on the verge of breakdown one year, simply due to the number of people who visited it. The bridge was repaired and renamed the Poohsticks Bridge.

130 People play hide-and-seek at a professional level too.

Hide and seek has always been a children's game. No one in their wildest dreams thought that it could be a sport or a competition too. Professor Hazaki of Nippon Sport Science University has started a new version of hide-and-seek in which the teams search for players that hide on a pitch measuring 65 × 65 ft. Professor Hazaki is now rooting for this sport to be included in the Olympics too.

131 There's an annual Quidditch World Cup.

Quidditch is a game that J.K. Rowling invented in her famous Harry Potter series. In the books, the game is played by wizards mounted on flying broomsticks. But it turns out that Quidditch is being played by muggles (non-magical people) too. People play this sport with a quaffle, broomsticks, hoops, bludgers and the coveted golden snitch. Participants hold brooms between their legs and throw balls around hoops. An International Quidditch Association has also been formed to hold the Quidditch World Cup annually.

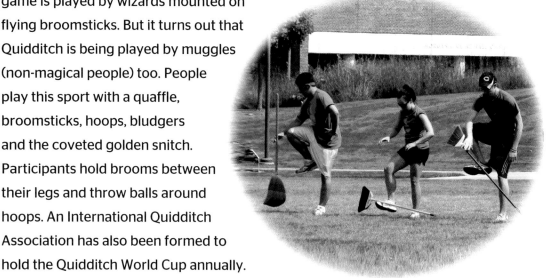

132 Bossaball is a mixture of four sports.

Bossaball is a hybrid sport that originated in Spain. It involves volleyball, beach soccer, gymnastics and capoeira. Capoeira is an Afro-Brazilian art form that combines music, dance with games and martial arts. Bossaball is played on an inflatable court which is specially designed for it. The court has a circular trampoline on each side of a net. It is a ball game between two teams, each consisting of three to five players. The referee of the game is known as a "samba referee" and he not only makes the various calls of the match but also plays music.

133 Basque Pelota is one of the fastest sports in the world.

Basque pelota is believed to be one of the fastest sports in the world that uses a ball, racquet and basket placed against a wall. It is believed that the game originated many years ago in Greece and was a famous sport of ancient civilisations. The game is played between two teams that are divided by a net or straight line. The players play with all the equipment and a bare hand. They use a hard ball in a small area, which moves at a very high speed.

134 Sepak Takraw is an Asian sport.

Can you imagine a sport that combines volleyball, soccer and gymnastics, and restricts players to use their hands throughout the game? Sepak Takraw is a popular, exciting, Asian sport that is gradually spreading throughout the world. The game is played on a court similar to a badminton court. The player passes the pass to the opponent, but is not allowed to use his/her arm. The use of any other part of the body is allowed, which in turn leads to brilliant jumps and flicks that give the sport its fun quotient.

135 Egg throwing is an Easter sport for some.

Early Christians adopted the egg as a symbol of rebirth at Easter. Egg throwing or egg tossing is a game associated with Easter. The delight of watching a human's failure to catch a tossed egg and get his/her body smeared with it has led to the development of egg throwing as a serious sport throughout the world.

Legend has it that egg throwing championships were held in churches in medieval Britain during Easter. In Germany, children played the sport on grassy meadows and found a way to spin the egg in such a way that it spun even after landing on the grass.

The organised sport of egg throwing is believed to have started around 1322 at Swaton village in Lincolnshire, England. It is said that the Abbot gave one egg to each peasant who attended the church. When the river near the church flooded and people could not go to church, the monks would hurl the eggs at the peasants on the other side. These are the humble beginnings of the now popular sport of egg throwing. The World Egg Throwing Federation was formed in 2004 to regulate the sport of egg throwing and its variations. The basic game involves a two member team; one hurls the egg in air and the other catches it.

136 There are world beard and moustache championships.

If you have a beard and a fancy moustache, you could participate in the next World Beard and Moustache Championships that are held annually in different cities of Europe. The history of this championship is controversial as the Italian delegation claims that the championship first started in Italy during the 1970s, whereas documents point towards the event being organised in a German village in 1990. The participants grow stylish beards and moustaches, and there are several variations in the championships that they can take part in.

137 Curling is a winter sport.

Curling is a winter sport that is often referred to as "chess on ice". Its origin can be traced to Scotland. It is a winter sport played with large, polished, heavy, granite stones on a rectangular sheet of ice. Originally an outdoor sport, it is now played indoors. The game involves teams of four players taking turns to slide the stones on ice towards a target. Points are awarded for a stone that is closer to the centre as compared to the other team's stone. The objective of the game is to accumulate as many points as possible.

138 The Cotswold Olimpick Games take place every year in England.

The Cotswold Olimpick Games are held annually at Dover's Hill, Chipping Campden, Gloucesershire, England. They were started by a local barrister named Captain Robert Dover, who believed that physical exercise was important for the army. Captain Rover also attempted to unite the different classes of society. Horse-racing, running, jumping, dancing, wrestling and fighting with swords were some of the events of the Cotswold Olimpick Games. The games were held in a natural amphitheatre, which is now known as Dover's Hill. The games attract thousands of visitors each year. The festivities include a torchlight procession, fireworks and a bonfire too.

The British Olympic Association believes that the Cotswold Olimpick Games are the historical thread that led to the creation of the Modern Olympics. The Civil War brought the Games to an end in 1642. The Cotswold Olimpick Games were first revived in 1660 and they were held on and off. The games were stopped in 1850 as they were held in a highly irregular manner. The second revival of the games was in 1951 during the Festival of Britain. The Cotswold Olimpick Games are a unique combination of rural and modern sporting events. Shin kicking and Tug O' War are the most popular events at these games.

139 "Demolition Derby" is a game in which drivers wreck each other's cars.

If you're a destructive person, perhaps you should consider a career as a professional demolition derbyist. The Demolition Derby event consists of five or more old cars. The drivers of these cars aim to destroy the opponent's vehicles by ramming into each other. The winner is the car that continues to operate till the end. Although serious injuries are rare, Demolition Derby has faced a lot of criticism as it is dangerous and involves the spilling of gasoline and oil, both harmful for the environment.

140 The "Milk Carton Regatta" is a water sport.

You must have heard about many water sports, but have you heard about the Milk Carton Regatta, a popular sport in the USA and Australia? The participants construct a boat entirely out of empty cartons and jugs. They race against each other in those boats. The Milk Carton Regatta aims to raise awareness about health and nutrition among students and adults. The competitions are held in Hawaii and Adelaide, Australia, and they are very famous.

141 Stair-climbing races are held all over the world.

You were probably aware that climbing the stairs is better for your health than taking the elevator. But did you know that it's actually played as a sport around the world? Participants take part in races and run up the stairs of the tallest towers and buildings in the world. Stair-climbing is one of the most gruelling and tough sports as the participants need to move their entire body weight vertically. Stair-climbing is gaining popularity as a sport because it burns twice the number of calories than any other sport and requires a shorter amount of time to achieve a workout of the same intensity.

142 Three-sided football is played with three teams.

Have you heard of a sport that has three teams in one match? Three-sided football, a variation of soccer, is one such sport that is played on a hexagonal pitch. The sport was devised by Asger Jorn. Three-sided football has three teams that play each other in a game of soccer. You'd think that the team with the most goals is the winner, but get ready to be surprised. The winner is the team that scores the least number of goals!

143 Street Luge is a dangerous game in Southern California.

Street Luge is a gravity-powered sport involving a street luge board or a sled that goes downhill on a road at a very fast speed. Street Luge originated in Southern California when skateboarders found that they achieved faster speeds if they were lying down on their skateboards. The participants race downhill only inches away from the ground at speeds of 60-160 km/h. The first professional Street Luge race was hosted by the US Skateboard Association in Signal Hill, California.

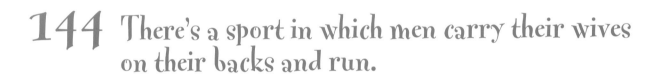

144 There's a sport in which men carry their wives on their backs and run.

Races have been around for eons now. But the Wife Carrying Festival takes them one step ahead. It is an annual sporting event that requires a man to carry his wife on his back for a distance of 253.5 m. The course of the race includes different surfaces like land and water, and has some obstacles too. The winning prize is beer—the amount of which is determined by the wife's weight!

145 Extreme ironing is another interesting sport.

Ironing is a rather tedious chore for most people. But some people have found a way to make it more interesting and even competitive. As the name suggests, extreme ironing is a sport in which the participants take ironing boards to extreme, unusual locations and iron clothes. For example, a forest, on top of a car or a hill, on top of statues, underwater, while parachuting or even in a cargo plane! Extreme ironing fans say that the sport was started by Phil Shaw in his back garden in Leicester, England.

146 Wood-chopping as a sport is more than 100 years old.

We all know that humans have been chopping wood since time immemorial for various purposes; from lighting a fire to making utensils, tools and jewellery. But do you know that wood-chopping as a sport has been played for more than a century now? Legend has it that the sport originated as the result of a bet between two men as to who could chop a tree faster. The first wood-chopping championship was held in 1891 in Tasmania. The sport is played in Australia, New Zealand, USA, Canada, United Kingdom, Spain and many other countries.

147 Surfing is one of the oldest sports known to humankind.

You probably thought that surfing is a modern sport that gained popularity recently. Well, you are mistaken. Surfing is believed to be one of the oldest sports known to humankind. The art of surfing is a complete blend of athleticism and the comprehension of nature's beauty and its sheer power. The idea of riding a wooden board originated 3,000 years ago in Polynesia. The fishermen discovered that it was faster to reach the shore with their fish if they rode on a wooden board.

When surfing actually transformed into a recreational sport is unclear. It is believed that during the 15th century, the royalty and the people of the Sandwich Isles enjoyed the sport of "he'enalu" or wave sliding to a great extent. Modern surfing as a sport emerged in the early 20th century.

ONCE UPON A TIME

Human beings began evolving more than 4 million years ago. Humans discovered how to write only 6,000 years ago. This means that we have no record of over 99% of human history! However, we have been able to find out a lot about human life by piecing together the information that we get from other sources, like the tools that humans used and excavated cities. Read on to find out about well-known and not so well-known historical facts.

148 Funerals were common even 60,000 years ago.

Neanderthal men lived on Earth about 1,30,000 years ago. Skulls and other remains of Neanderthal men along with remnants of flowers have recently been discovered. This means that Neanderthal men had customs and rituals for the dead. Unlike modern times, the burial tradition during the era of Neanderthal man didn't involve digging a deep pit. Instead, the body was placed on the ground and covered with mud, stones, plants and flowers. Sometimes, the corpses were even left in the open on a raised platform or amidst the plants.

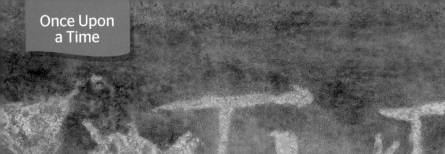

149 The Stone Age lasted for more than 2 million years.

The Stone Age is divided into the Paleolithic Era and the Neolithic Era. The Paleolithic Era is the Old Stone Age, while the Neolithic Era is the New Stone Age. During these ages, humans used stone to hunt, carve the hunted meat and grow crops.

Some of the tools that came to be used in this era were spearheads, flints and hand axes. The need to make such tools arose because human hands were not strong enough for hunting or digging the ground. What differentiated humans from other animals was the possession of opposable thumbs. This means that your thumbs move in different directions from the rest of your fingers. Press your thumbs against the forefingers on the same hand. This tiny motion is the reason why you can write and your pet dog can't.

There are a lot of cave paintings that survived from the Stone Age. The oldest cave paintings can be found at the Bhimbetka rock shelters in India. They date back to almost 30,000 years!

150 Mesopotamia is called the "cradle of civilisation".

Situated in present-day Iraq, the Mesopotamian civilisation is one of the earliest known to humankind. The land between the Rivers Tigris and Euphrates is known as "Mesopotamia". This was where humans first started farming and agriculture. Along with agriculture, the Mesopotamians also started building a very primitive kind of society. Around 3500 BCE, the first cities of the world—Ur, Uruk and Eridu—made an appearance in Mesopotamia. Most of the first inventions were made here, including the wheel.

151 The Sumerians invented the wheel.

The wheel is often referred to as one of humankind's greatest inventions. The invention is credited to the Sumerians, who lived in Mesopotamia. They noticed that it was easier to roll a round log than it was to drag a flat plank. They started experimenting with other round objects and that's how the wheel was invented! They used it to transport heavy objects from one place to another.

152 Cleopatra wasn't born Egyptian.

Cleopatra is known as an extremely beautiful
Egyptian Queen. She was born around
68 BCE into the Ptolemaic dynasty
in Egypt. She was a descendant of
the Macedonian Greeks, who were
ruling Egypt during those times.
Her father passed away in 51 BCE,
after which the task of ruling the
country lay upon her and her
brother. She was just 17 at the time.
The Ptolemaic dynasty followed the
Greek culture in those days. However,
Cleopatra decided to honour Egyptian
traditions and was actually the first in her
family to learn the Egyptian language.

153 The earliest pillow dates back to 7000 BCE.

Pillows may seem like some kind of frivolous, modern-day luxury, but even
ancient civilisations were aware of the comfort that a raised head
offered while sleeping. The oldest pillow was found in
Mesopotamia, which is located in modern-day Iraq,
dating back to 7000 BCE. This pillow was a block
of stone with a slightly curved top to pose as a
headrest! Even the Ancient Egyptians liked
sleeping with a pillow under their head. But
strangely, though they had the luxury of a
soft, cushy pillow, they preferred to sleep
on pillows made of stone! Why they chose
to do so remains a mystery.

154 Egyptians loved board games enough to have them in their tombs.

Ancient Egyptians are known for many things—from pyramids to hieroglyphs to cat worship. But few are aware that board games were considered to be common as far back as 3500 BCE in Egypt and were unearthed from tombs! The most common Egyptian board game was called Senet. It was similar to Snakes and Ladders. The board had symbols depicting good and bad luck. The aim was to reach the destination without falling prey to the pitfalls. The person who got "home" safely, won.

155 English is written from the left to the right because of the Greek.

Have you ever wondered why Hebrew and Arabic are written from right to left, Chinese is written from top to bottom and English from left to right? It's because of ancient Greek scholars. They experimented by putting words on tablets in various ways and tried reading them. They found that reading from left to right was the easiest. When the Greeks were eventually conquered by the Romans, they took on this practice too. Since Latin is the root of English and all other Western languages, they are also written horizontally from left to right.

156 It took years to decipher hieroglyphs.

Hieroglyphs are the oldest, most complex form of writing. They are so elaborate that Egyptologists took years to decipher the meaning behind all the symbols.

All the monuments, tombs and other stone structures in Egypt are peppered with hieroglyphics. Hieroglyphs weren't always written in the same direction. They could either be written from left to right or right to left. They were sometimes even written from top to bottom. There are no vowels in Egyptian writing, which confused all the archeologists and Egyptologists.

Moreover, there were two kinds of hieroglyphics. "lideograms" were hieroglyphs where the symbol stood for the word; for example, the drawing of man stood for the word "man". Then there were "phonograms", which represented the sound of the word they depicted.

The Ancient Egyptians didn't use any punctuation and didn't have spaces between their words. There were more than 700 hieroglyphs in the Egyptian alphabet!

157 The Spartans subjected their children to extraordinary tests of fitness.

The Spartans were a race that prided themselves on their strength and prowess at war. And they left no stone unturned to ensure that they remained so. All newborn Spartans were first presented to a council of ministers. If they found any physical defect or deformity in the child, it was abandoned by the State. The parents were forced to leave the child by a hillside. However, a lot of babies that were abandoned by the hillside were later rescued and brought up by strangers.

The ordeal of being born in Sparta didn't end there! Babies who survived were tested further and put through rigorous training by being bathed in wine and then left alone in the dark. Spartan babies were expected to be fearless and strong enough to fight against diseases. Crying children were often ignored by their parents because it was believed that this made them tougher.

Spartan men had only one occupation by default—that of a soldier. They compulsorily had to serve their country till the age of 60.

158 The Aztecs kept tax records on tree trunks and deer skin.

The Aztecs are an ancient civilisation that originated in Mexico in the 13th century. They have gone down in history as a bunch of barbaric warmongers, but they were actually a complex society. They had their own pictorial language called "N'ahuatl". They used barks of trees and deer skins to record information like tax records and historical records. They were also a very artistic civilisation. They were into poetry, sculpting and painting. The most popular art form was art designed for their warriors, which was often tattooed onto them as a mark of honour.

159 Ancient Chinese bound their daughter's feet.

The Ancient Chinese thought that small feet were pretty. To ensure that their daughters had the smallest feet possible, in the 10th century, Chinese families resorted to binding their feet once the girl turned six. The girl's feet were soaked in a mixture of herbs and animal blood. After her toe nails were cut, her feet were massaged and wrapped tightly in long, silk bandages, thereby stunting the foot's growth. It was a painful tradition that often caused deformities.

160 The Indus Valley civilisation had a population of over 5 million.

The Indus Valley was excavated in the 1920s and this impressive ancient civilisation was made known to the world. This civilisation is believed to have started evolving around 3300 BCE and is said to have housed more than five million people during its prime.

The most striking part about this civilisation was its drainage system. It was so well-planned and well-laid that even today, engineers are in awe of it. Apart from the drainage, even the cities were well-planned, with organised irrigation and plumbing facilities. Mohenjo-Daro is the most prominent city of this civilisation. The Great Bath, religious structures and huge granaries were located in the upper part of the city. The residential area was laid out neatly in the lower part. The occupation of people here was usually farming or trading.

The Indus Valley civilisation flourished for about 1,000 years and then faded away. While some believe that a severe drought wiped out the state, others feel that Aryan invaders are to be blamed.

The Indus Valley Civilisation had no rulers and there were very few rules that divided the society. It was almost a classless society where everyone was considered equal.

161 Japanese monks believed that mummification would lead to enlightenment.

We are all aware of Egyptian mummies. But Japanese monks would mummify themselves too—except that it was a much more elaborate and torturous procedure. They believed that successful mummification led to enlightenment. In order to be mummified, the monk would first have to eat only nuts and seeds and undergo vigorous activity for three years. During this time, he would lose all his body fat. After that, the monk would start drinking a poisonous tea made from the sap of the Urushi tree. This would make the monk lose all his body fluid through vomiting and diarrhoea. It would also make his body too poisonous to be eaten by maggots. Then, he would lock himself in a coffin that was slightly larger than him. He would breathe through a narrow pipe that was provided and keep ringing a bell. The bell indicated that the monk was alive inside the coffin. Once the bell stopped ringing, the pipe was removed and the coffin sealed. After another three years, the coffin was opened. If the monk was successfully mummified, he was believed to have attained enlightenment. Only a few of the monks actually got mummified. Most bodies just decomposed.

This practise began about 1,000 years ago and is now outlawed by the Japanese government.

162 The tradition of duels began in ancient Europe.

In ancient Europe, might actually was right! Back then, when there were no courtrooms, lawyers or law, judgment was passed based on a person's duelling skills!

By the Middle Ages, duelling didn't remain just a matter of justice, but actually became a sport. Knights wanted to show off by holding tournaments among themselves. Duelling as a sport travelled to the USA along with the first settlers in the 1600s. It remained popular throughout history and was attended by many people.

163 Some Tibetans believed in "sky burial".

According to this practice, the body is left out in the open for vultures to feed on. Tibetans believe that once the person is dead, his soul moves on, leaving the body behind. The body is allowed to disintegrate and return to nature. Tibet's rough terrain doesn't allow them to dig graves. There is also not much wood to burn the bodies, which is why leaving the bodies out in the open is convenient.

164 Ancient Rome had shopping malls that were four floors high.

The world's first shopping mall was Trajan's market in Ancient Rome. It was four storeys high and had about 150 shops and offices! It is believed that Trajan's Market was built in 100-110 CE by Apollodorous of Damascus. It now stands as a ruin at the opposite end of the Colosseum, but one can still sense the grandeur it once exuded. The shops and apartments were built in a multi-level structure, several of which are still intact. Traces of marble flooring and the remains of a library are still visible.

165 Paper money originated in China.

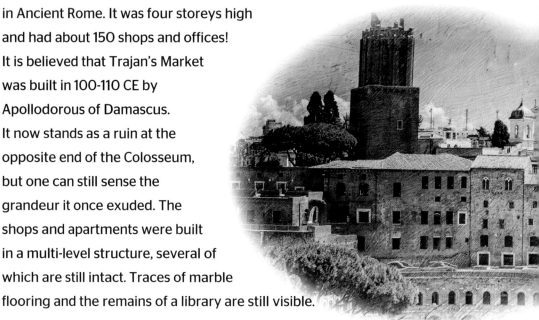

It was in the 7th century, during the Tang dynasty, that paper money came to be used. People got tired of carrying the load of copper coins everywhere. In cases of large transactions, lots of manpower was required to carry the bundles of coins. Traders and merchants then began depositing "certificates" that were worth a certain amount of money. Paper money evolved from these certificates. As they were so much lighter to carry, they were also called "flying money".

166 Pompeii is so well preserved; graffiti on its walls can still be read.

Pompeii was a thriving city that was swallowed by a volcanic eruption. In fact, because of the hot lava that settled over it, it was buried exactly as it was and has been preserved for all these years! The bodies of some people have been found in exactly the same position as they were when they got buried. Buildings, shops and homes are also preserved exactly as they were. It is believed that the eruption occurred around 80 CE. However, before the eruption, Pompeii was a thriving city with a government and infrastructure. The city shows a complex structure with a complex water system, amphitheatre, gymnasium and port.

Pompeii is believed to have been an attractive vacation spot even back then. Archeologists have found plenty of public party spots, an arena, gladiator's barracks, restaurants and even a hotel. The city is so well preserved that even to-let signs and graffiti on the walls can be read!

In 62 CE, an earthquake hit the city of Pompeii. The city suffered from massive damages and it took many years to rebuild it. This made a lot of its citizens move away to other Roman cities.

167 Marco Polo wrote *The Travels of Marco Polo* when he was in jail.

Many people have heard about Marco Polo's love for travel and adventure, but not many are aware that he actually led a small band of people into war. Three years after he returned from his famous journey in 1293, a war was raging between Venice and Genoa, a rival Italian state. He led a small band into Genoa to fight the war. He was arrested there. While he was in jail, he befriended a fellow inmate, Rustichello of Pisa, known for his romantic verses. Marco Polo shared the stories of his travels with him and he turned them into the famous book.

168 The longest war in history was called the Hundred Years' War.

Though the name of the war is the "Hundred Years' War", it is misleading because the war actually lasted for 116 years. It was fought between England and France over the succession of the French throne. It began in 1337 and ended in 1453. France was fighting to get rid of British influence, while the British were fighting to retain control. Lots of monarchs changed on both sides from the start to the end of the war. Finally, by the end, most of the French territories were free from British influence.

169 Yi Sun-sin, a Korean admiral, won a war with only 13 ships.

Yi Sun-sin is one of the most revered Korean admirals and generals in Korean history. He successfully defended Korea from Japanese invasion with only 13 ships. The Japanese had 133. Though he never received any naval training before the war, he is one of the most successful and celebrated admirals. He remained undefeated in all his 23 naval battles! He died in 1598 during the Battle of Noryang. The Japanese were about to be defeated when he was hit. His famous dying words were, "The battle is at its height...beat my war drums...do not announce my death."

170 Passengers on the Mayflower were called "pilgrims".

The Mayflower was a ship that crossed the Atlantic Ocean through a severe storm in 1620. As all the passengers managed to survive the adverse conditions, it was believed that the hand of God was protecting them. According to the story, the Mayflower was actually a merchant ship carrying wine and dry goods. When a neighbouring boat called "Speedwell" started leaking, its 102 passengers were safely transferred to the Mayflower.

171 In the 1600s, tax was levied in the form of fur in Serbia.

Money has come a long way from its humble beginnings. During its journey from copper coins to our bank accounts, money went through some strange phases. When Russians landed in Serbia in the 1600s, they realised that the natives owned beautiful, exquisite furs. Slowly, more Russians started pouring in and then began the historic fur trade. Money started pouring into Serbia from North America. Fur even came to be called "soft gold".

By the 17th century, this trade had become so prevalent that the government imposed taxes which were payable only by fur. This way, a certain amount of fur always stayed in the country.

172 The French Revolution went on for 10 years.

The French Revolution resulted in a makeover of the French political system. It inspired all subsequent revolutions, including the American Revolution and India's freedom struggle. The French Revolution began in 1789 and ended in the late 1790s. Legend says that when hungry people at the gates were clamouring for bread, Queen Mary Antoinette said, "If they have no bread, let them have cake."

While this is probably just an exaggerated tale, it does highlight the disparity between the ruling class and its subjects. The royal family was eventually guillotined.

173 A sweaty apple slice played an important role in 19th century Austrian dating.

During the 19th century in rural Austria, dances were organised for large groups of boys and girls gathered together. The girls would dance with slices of apple under their armpits. When the music stopped playing, they would offer the sweat-soaked apple slices to the partner of their choice. If the feeling was mutual, the boy would have to eat the slice before they could go on a date!

174 The shortest war in history lasted for 38 minutes.

On 27th August, 1896, a war was fought between the United Kingdom and the Zanzibar sultanate. The conflict lasted for less than 40 minutes and is said to be the shortest war in history. The cause of the war was that the Zanzibaris wanted to elect one Sultan as their leader and the British wanted another. About 2,800 Zanzibaris defended the palace against the British, of whom 500 were killed.

Most of the Zanzibaris were civilians and slaves. In a short span of time, while only one British sailor was injured, around 500 Zanzibaris were killed.

175 The "Trail of Tears" is a journey in history.

In 1835, the Supreme Court of America granted the native tribes of Cherokee permission to stay in a part of Georgia. But some years later, a small group of Cherokees signed a treaty that allowed the USA to displace them from their residential land. They were to be sent to Oklahoma. American troops moved in and forced the Cherokees out. The journey from Georgia to Oklahoma was a difficult one. Many tears were shed during this journey, leading it to be named the "Trail of Tears".

176 "Monopoly" board games helped thousands of prisoners escape during World War II.

During World War II, many American and British soldiers were taken as prisoners in German prisons. They devised a cunning way to smuggle escaping tools into the prison.

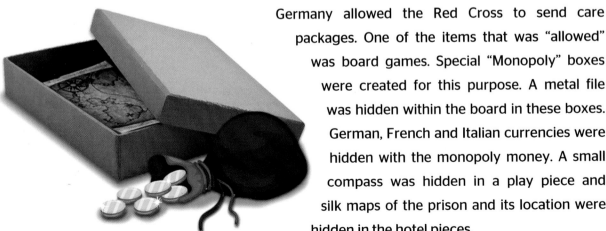

Germany allowed the Red Cross to send care packages. One of the items that was "allowed" was board games. Special "Monopoly" boxes were created for this purpose. A metal file was hidden within the board in these boxes. German, French and Italian currencies were hidden with the monopoly money. A small compass was hidden in a play piece and silk maps of the prison and its location were hidden in the hotel pieces.

177 A monk burned himself as a form of protest in Vietnam.

On 11th June, 1963, Buddhist monks had been protesting against the Diem regime for more than a month. A procession of 350 monks and nuns arrived outside the Cambodian Embassy in Saigaon. Thich Quang Duc, a monk, put a cushion in the centre of the road and sat on it. The other monks formed a circle around him and poured around 18 l of fuel on him. The monk calmly sat there, chanting his prayers. He then stopped chanting, struck a match and dropped it on himself.

The monk caught fire immediately. Many onlookers tried to stop him but were stopped by the circle of monks. The crowd stood horrified as the monk burned to death. It is said that not a sound escaped his lips throughout his self-immolation and that he had nothing but a calm expression on his face.

On the night of the burning, hundreds of Vietnamese claimed to see the face of a crying Buddha in the sunset.

178 The protests against the war on Iraq were the largest anti-war protests in history.

The Iraq war was an eight-year war between the USA and Iraq that began on 19th March, 2003. The protests against the war began in 2002 itself, when the US army was planning the invasion. Many thought that the war was unnecessary. Protests were held in many cities all over the world, often coordinated to occur simultaneously. There were protests in England, Italy, France and USA, among others. In Rome, there was a 3 million people protest that went into the Guinness Book of World Records as the biggest anti-war protest in human history. It was estimated that around 36 million people participated.

179 Nepal has the most unique flag in the world.

Every flag in the country is a different combination of colours and shapes—but they are all rectangular. That's why the flag of Nepal is so unique—it's the only flag that isn't rectangular! The flag is made of two overlapping triangles. There is a moon on the top triangle and a Sun on the triangle below. The two triangles represent the Himalayan mountains and the two major religions of the country—Buddhism and Hinduism. They represent hope that the country will last as long as the Sun and moon shine.

180 Hitler wanted to be an artist.

The atrocities committed by Adolf Hitler are enough to send shivers down many spines even today. There are others who are in awe of his administration. But surprising as it may sound, he actually wanted to be an artist! He had applied to the Vienna Academy of Arts, twice. But after his parents passed away, he joined the German Army. He survived World War I and quickly rose up the ranks. The rest of his life story is known to most. We also know that he committed suicide to end his life, but most don't know that it was the day after he got married to his girlfriend, Eva Braun, on 30th April, 1945.

181 Alexander the Great was epileptic.

Alexander the Great is known for establishing one of the greatest empires in the ancient world. His empire extended from modern day Greece to Pakistan. He was born on 20th July, 356 BCE. He died after 12 years of constant military campaigning. He was born in Macedon, as the son of King Phillip II. A lesser known fact about him is that he had epilepsy, a disorder that causes a person to have many seizures. During the time of Alexander the Great, epilepsy was known as "the sacred disease" because it was believed that everyone who had seizures were either possessed by evil spirits or touched by the Gods.

182 Abraham Lincoln was the tallest president in American history.

Abraham Lincoln is well-known for being the American president who abolished slavery. He is also known for his progressive views on feminism and his extreme honesty. What he is not very well-known for is his position as the tallest American president. At 6 ft 4 inches, he ties with Lyndon Johnson. It is now believed that Lincoln might have suffered from the Marfan syndrome, a genetic disorder in which the affected people tend to be unusually tall with long limbs and thin, long fingers.

183 Roosevelt continued giving a speech even after he was shot.

On 14th October, 1912, former American president Theodore Roosevelt was shot in the chest just as he was about to give a speech. He insisted that he would not go to the hospital until he finished the speech. He began his speech by saying, "Friends, I shall ask you to be as quiet as possible. I don't know whether you fully understand that I have just been shot." He then proceeded to remove a paper on which he had written the speech from his chest pocket. It was covered in blood and had a large hole through it. It had slowed down the bullet enough to keep it from killing him!

184 The great Pharaoh Ramses II was the first king in history to sign a peace treaty.

Pharaoh Ramses II, also known as Ramses the Great, ruled Egypt for 67 years during the 12th century BCE and was known as "Ramses the Great". He is one of the best-known pharaohs in history and Egypt reached an overwhelming state of prosperity during his reign. He was also a great peacemaker. He was the first king in history to sign a peace treaty with his enemies, the Hittites. The treaty covers the settlement of disputes and mutual economic aid among other things. Its copy can be seen at the General Assembly building of the United Nations.

185 Jesus Christ's real name was Yeshua.

Jesus Christ's birth name was actually Yeshua. In Hebrew, this means "salvation". The English equivalent of Yeshua is Joshua. But he is still referred to as Jesus by most. This is because the Bible came to the English speaking world through the Greeks, not directly from Hebrew. When translated into Greek, they translated Jesus as "Iesous", pronounced as "eeyasoos". The Greek Iesous was translated into English as Jesus. Further, Christ was not his surname. "Christ" means the "messiah". It was a title given to him. Back in those days, people in Israel didn't have surnames. They were simply known by their father's name.

186 Christopher Columbus didn't actually think that Earth was flat.

A popular myth says that when Christopher Columbus set out on his expedition, everyone thought that the world was flat and that he would eventually fall off the edge of Earth. But this is not true. In fact, way back in the 6th century BCE, Pythagoras wrote that Earth was a sphere. Educated people in Columbus' time were well aware that falling off the edge of Earth wasn't possible.

When Columbus announced that he wished to discover a sea route to Asia, the main debate was around the circumference of Earth. Most scholars believed that Earth was too large to reach Asia without a stop to restock on food and water, and that the crew would perish on the voyage with nothing to eat and drink. This was technically true, because Columbus didn't actually reach Asia, he discovered America instead!

When Christopher Columbus reached the Caribbean, he thought he had reached India, which is why he called the natives "Red Indians".

IN THE JUNGLE

The natural world is a lot more interesting than you think. With more than 3,00,000 species of plants and close to 77,00,000 species of animals, some creatures are bizarre enough to put science fiction to shame!

187 Some plants enjoy non-vegetarian food.

Some plants feed on insects and other small animals. There are more than 600 species of carnivorous plants, though the most well-known is probably the Pitcher plant. It gets the name because of its beautiful pitcher shaped leaf trap. The Pitcher plant's leaves are folded into deep pits that serve as traps. They are slippery, hollow ditches filled with digestive enzymes that look like a dark liquid. Prey such as insects and small animals attempt to drink this liquid and get sucked into it instead. Once the victim falls in and the trap door closes, digestive enzymes similar to those in the human stomach slowly consume the insect. When dinner is over, the plant ejects the remains and is ready to trap again.

188 Blue whales are the largest animals.

The largest animal is the blue whale. It is about 100 ft long and can weigh up to 150 tonnes! Roughly 17 people would have to stand on top of each other to measure up to the length of a blue whale.

A blue whale's tongue weighs more than a male elephant. The largest blue whale ever measured was a female weighing 1,71,000 kg and measuring over 90 ft long. Though the ancient dinosaurs were massive, they were never as big as the blue whale. Most scientists agree that the blue whale is the largest creature to have ever lived on Earth!

No one can say for sure since dinosaurs no longer exist. But some scientists say that a group of dinosaurs, known as "sauropods", actually measured more than 110 ft, beating the blue whale!

189 The most poisonous animal is the jellyfish.

Even though snakes are the most feared poisonous animals, jellyfish are the most dangerous ones! They live underwater and are found all over the world. In spite of their name, jellyfish are not actually fish. They belong to an animal group called "Cnidaria". They are related to corals and anemones. Jellyfish have long tentacles, which are their stingers. A sting from the box jellyfish can be very dangerous. The small box jellyfish is the size of an average human thumbnail, but is the deadliest animal on the planet. This infamous jellyfish has frighteningly powerful venom that instantly stuns and sometimes even kills its prey.

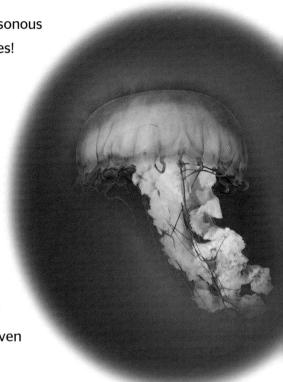

190 A bamboo can grow up to 3 ft in 24 hours.

The bamboo is the fastest growing plant on the planet. The record for the fastest bamboo growth in a 24-hour period was 47 inches, which is almost 4 ft! Though its height may tempt you to think differently, bamboo is actually a kind of grass which grows almost all over the world, except for very cold regions.

Bamboo was first used to make everyday items in China. Evidence of bamboo being used to make articles such as arrows, books, paper and as building material dates back to 7,000 years!

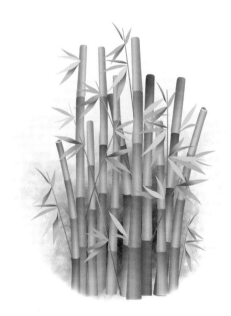

191 A woodpecker's tongue wraps itself around its skull when retracted.

The red-bellied woodpecker's tongue is so long that it is at least thrice the length of its beak. When pulled back in, the tongue wraps itself around the skull. This woodpecker needs its super long tongue to find food. It pecks on a tree at the rate of 24 km/h. While doing this, it pushes its elongated tongue deep into the hole, searching for small bugs or insects. Once it finds one, it pierces its prey with its tongue, which is covered in tiny, sharp spikes. The woodpecker then pulls back the tongue with its prey and proceeds to eat it.

192 Bees can calculate distances and angles in their head.

Bees communicate with each other about where to find food, a new home and other such things by doing a certain "dance". Lots of scientists have been conducting experiments to find out the extent of bees' abilities. They discovered that bees can actually take into account the roundness of Earth and fly past obstacles by calculating the angle between them and their food. So basically, bees are like tiny math geniuses that are capable of performing complicated calculations without calculators!

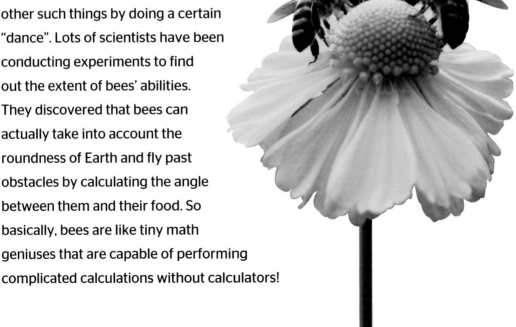

193 There's a jellyfish that ages backwards.

Most jellyfish don't live for more than a few months, except for one called Turritopsis Nutricula, found in the Caribbean Sea. This jellyfish can reverse the aging process, which means that it's practically immortal! When this jellyfish is in its larva stage, it attaches itself to a sturdy surface and grows while it is still attached. It detaches itself from the surface and becomes a free-floating jellyfish only after a very long time. During times of prolonged hunger, it can actually transform itself back to a larva stage and start the process all over again!

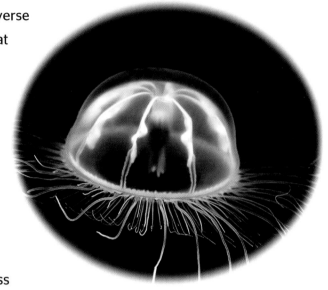

194 The pistol shrimp is one of the loudest animals on the planet.

This tiny little critter barely measures 5 cm, which means that it's hardly longer than your little finger. But don't be fooled by its tiny size—it can produce a sound that's louder than a jet engine! The shrimp has a claw that is shaped like a pistol. One part of the claw is fixed, but the other part moves backwards into a right-angled position. When the shrimp snaps these two shut, it is capable of shooting out water at a speed of 100 km/h. This creates a bubble that bursts with a snap so loud, it can easily break an aquarium glass!

195 Dolphins sleep with only half a brain at a time.

Dolphins can't breathe unconsciously the way we do. Since they are mammals and not fish, they do not have gills. This means that they can't breathe underwater. They need to keep coming up to the surface of the water to breathe (which is why they jump out of the water). This is why they can't be truly unconscious when they sleep.

But being mammals, their brain does need to rest every once in a while. That is why while half the dolphin's brain is asleep, the other half is conscious and making sure that the dolphin is breathing and alive. Dolphins keep switching conscious sides of their brain. They remain in this state for approximately eight hours a day. This way, they make sure that they are alive and breathing while resting their brain.

"Killer whales" are actually dolphins. In fact, they are the largest member of the dolphin family.

196 The copepod is the world's strongest animal.

Copepods are small animals that live in the sea and in freshwater. They are very small, barely 1 mm long. Copepods are also the world's fastest animal, being able to jump at the rate of about half a metre per second. Relative to their size, they are stronger than any other living animal. In fact, they're even stronger than any mechanical motor produced. This does not mean that they can carry very heavy things or are stronger than large animals—it just means that in comparison to their size, they are incredibly strong. So, if all animals were to be the size of a copepod, the copepod would be the strongest.

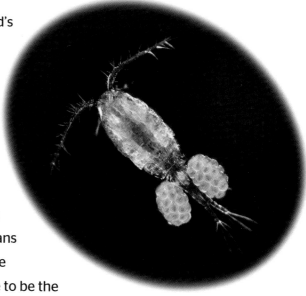

197 South African earthworms can grow up to 22 ft long.

A certain species of South African earthworm, Microchaetus skeadi, can grow to be as long as 22 ft! The average length of a South African earthworm is about 6 ft.

The longest one found so far, which was 22 ft, was found by the roadside in 1967.

As gross as it seems, this earthworm is actually quite important for the soil in South Africa. It is believed that the soil is so fertile only because of this ginormous earthworm.

198 The Amazon provides 20% of the oxygen in the world.

The Amazon forest is sprawled over 60,00,000 km² in the north-eastern part of the South American continent. The forest is also called the "lungs of Earth", because it provides 20% of the oxygen that the world needs. Scientists estimate that more than half the species of wildlife in the world can be found in the Amazon. It has 500 kinds of mammals, 175 types of lizards, more than 300 species of reptiles and about one-third of the birds found all over the world. It experiences 9 ft of rain every year and most of the water from rainfall gets used by the foliage found in the area.

199 Planktons form the base of the food chain in the ocean.

Planktons are plants that float along with the ocean currents. The word "plankton" is derived from the Greek word "planktos", which means drifter or wanderer. We don't give these microorganisms half the credit they deserve! Without them, there would be no life on Earth! About 50% of the oxygen we breathe has been contributed to the atmosphere by planktons. Besides, planktons are food for other animals called zooplanktons. These, in turn, fall prey to other animals and fish in the sea. You can see how plankton forms the base of the food chain in the ocean.

200 Butterflies can taste with their feet.

Butterflies' taste sensors are located on their feet. They can taste their food just by standing on it! They don't have a mouth or teeth to help them eat. Instead, they have a long, straw-like structure called a "proboscis" which they use to drink nectar and juices. But there are no taste sensors on the proboscis.

By standing on a leaf, the butterfly can taste it to see if the leaf it is sitting on will be good to lay eggs on or not. Only certain leaves are good as food. Once it finds the perfect leaf, the butterfly's meal begins!

201 Bees are an endangered species.

The population of bees all around the world is declining. While this doesn't seem very alarming, some scientists say that human beings will disappear four years after bees because bees help pollinate flowers. Without bees, we wouldn't have any plants!

Scientists think that a particular chemical in pesticides is causing bees to become disoriented and lose their way. Unable to find their way back to the hive, the bees eventually die.

202 The Angler fish uses a fishing rod to catch its prey.

The Angler fish is a brown coloured fish that is found in tropical environments. It is about 8 inches to 3 ft in length and weighs about 50 kg. But what is most fascinating about this fish is its method of catching other fish. It has a structure protruding from the top of its head, like a fishing rod. At the end of this structure is a light, which dangles right in front of its mouth. The fish uses this as bait, much like fishermen use worms at the end of their rod. The prey gets attracted to the light. Once the prey is close enough, the Angler fish pounces on the prey and snaps its jaws shut.

203 Piranhas can eat a cow in a few minutes.

Piranhas are one of the most dangerous species of fish on Earth. They often eat up their prey in a matter of seconds, before their prey even realises it is being eaten. Piranhas have very sharp teeth and are found in the rivers of South America. They hunt in groups known as schools and one school can contain as many as 1,000 fish in one meal! Though they usually feed on other animals, in case of a food shortage, they can even turn into cannibals. This means that they can eat other piranhas to survive.

204 Frogs breathe through their skin.

Frogs can actually breathe through their lungs and their skin. When they are on land, they breathe like all other land animals—through their nostrils. But when they are completely submerged underwater, they can breathe through their skin. Their blood vessels are very close to the surface of their skin. Their skin is covered with a thin layer that absorbs oxygen from the water directly into the blood vessels. Carbon dioxide is removed from the body in the same way, through their skin.

205 Leatherback Sea Turtles are the largest turtles on Earth.

These massive turtles have actually stood the test of time, considering the fact that they've been around since the time of the dinosaurs! They are carnivorous turtles with an average lifespan of around 45 years. They can grow up to 7 ft and weigh up to 916 kg. This means that they weigh almost as much as a full grown giraffe! They live in the cold waters of the Atlantic and Pacific Oceans. But their population is dwindling because of water pollution and other threats.

206 The King Cobra's venom is so poisonous that it can kill an elephant in a single bite.

The King Cobra is mostly found in the forests of Southeast Asia. It is the longest venomous snake in the world. It is often found in forests and near water. It is at ease on land and in water. It can even move quickly on trees. An average King Cobra is 13 ft long, though some even grow up to 18 ft! A single bite from a King Cobra is enough to kill an elephant or 20 grown men. Venom from a King Cobra can kill a person in 45 minutes. But King Cobras don't usually attack unless they feel threatened and barely five people die from cobra bites each year.

When a King Cobra feels threatened, it raises its head high off the ground and prepares to strike. The sides of its head will flare out to create a menacing hood. They may also let out a fairly loud hiss that almost sounds like a growl. Cobras generally eat other smaller snakes. But they sometimes also eat lizards and other small mammals. Their life span is about 20 years.

The mongoose is the only natural predator of the King Cobra because it is immune to its venom.

207 Hummingbirds beat their wings 60-80 times per second.

Hummingbirds flap their wings so fast that you can't even see them! In fact, the humming sound that hummingbirds make comes from their rapid wing flapping. Hummingbirds have long beaks that they use to obtain nectar from long, tubular flowers. By changing the pattern in which they flap their wings, they can fly forward, backward, upward, downward and even hover in one place. They are the only birds with this unique ability. But this ability is very important for their survival because they suck nectar from delicate flowers where there are usually no solid branches to sit on.

208 The oldest tree is 9,550 years old.

The oldest tree on Earth was found in the Dalarna Province of Sweden in 2004. It is a 13-foot-tall lone Norway spruce or the "Christmas tree". It is said to have taken root as a conifer during the end of the last Ice Age. The spruce was traditionally used as a Christmas tree in European homes. Normally, the spruce is expected to live for 600 years, but it has the ability to produce a new stem upon the death of an old stem, thereby increasing its life expectancy. This means that even though the trunk and stems of the tree may not have witnessed the end of the Ice Age, its 9,550-year-old roots have definitely been there, done that!

209 The World's tiniest tree is the Dwarf Willow.

The smallest tree in the world is the Dwarf Willow, found in Greenland. It can reach a height of just 5 cm. But it does spread itself out. It is also known as Snowbed Willow and Least Willow. It survives in the harsh arctic and subarctic environments around the North Atlantic Ocean. It has round, shiny, green leaves that are 1–2 cm long and quite broad.

210 The World's tallest tree is called Hyperion.

The redwoods, found in California, are the tallest trees in the world. These trees easily reach heights of 300 ft. But the tallest tree is named Hyperion. It was discovered in 2006 and is 379 ft tall. That's as tall as a building with 28 floors!

Other giant redwoods include Helios, which is slightly shorter than Hyperion, at 374.3 ft, as well as Icarus at 371 ft and Daedalus at 363.4 ft.

Redwoods usually live for around 500 to 700 years, though some have been recorded to be more than 2,000 years old!

211 Insects follow patterns on petals.

Most flowers have patterns of lines on their petals. These patterns act as a guide for insects to move towards the glands that produce nectar. These glands are usually near the base of the petals. How are we not able to see all these lines and patterns? That's because these flowers display the patterns in the UV rays that they reflect. Since we don't have ultraviolet vision, we can't see these lines. Insects can see ultraviolet rays, which is how they see nectar guides while we only see plain-coloured petals.

212 The largest single flower is the Rafflesia.

The Rafflesia flower grows in Indonesia. It can grow up to 3 ft long and weigh 11 kg. Its petals are red with faint yellow spots. There is a big disk in the middle of the flower with a 1-foot diameter. Though the flower is so huge, its seeds are quite small. The Rafflesia has no roots, leaves or stems. It needs only a few days to bloom. When it has just bloomed, its strong fragrance spreads far and wide. After four days, it starts withering and gives off an equally strong stench, attracting flies and insects. Within a few days, the beautiful flower turns into a sticky mush.

213 Antarctica is the only spider-free zone in the world.

Spiders are resilient creatures that can survive in almost any kind of climate. In fact, there are an estimated 50,000 spiders per acre of green land! Antarctica is the only area where they do not live. They can live just about anywhere—including on trees, plants, grass blades and backyards!

Most spiders are found on land and even in the driest of areas. Some live at the edges of lakes and ponds. The largest spider ever found had a 28-cm leg span! That's one massive spider!

214 The oldest-known animal in the world was 507 years old.

In 2006, scientists discovered a clam in Iceland. They can find out the age of a clam by counting the number of rings it has on its shell. Scientists estimated that this particular clam was 507 years old. They named it Ming, because when the clam was born, the Ming dynasty was ruling in China! Most clams live for very long periods of time. 200 and 300-year-old clams are quite common. But a 500-year-old clam—now that's REALLY old!

215 A notch in a tree will remain the same distance from the ground as the tree grows.

Though you may expect that a notch on a tree would be further away from the ground as the tree grows, this isn't the case. This means that if you hammer a nail in a tree trunk about 3 ft from the ground, it will always remain at 3 ft, no matter how much the tree has grown. The reason for this is actually quite simple. While growth cells are located in all parts of animals' bodies, growth cells are only located at the tips of the branches of trees. This means that only the tips of the tree grow.

216 Snails can sleep for three years at a time.

Snails are animals that need moisture to stay alive. But many snails live in very dry climates, so they have developed a few tricks to stay alive. One of these tricks is extremely long hibernation, which means that they can actually nap for three hours at a stretch if the climate is unfavourable. They've adapted in many other ways too. They are mostly nocturnal, which means that they are awake at night and asleep during the day, avoiding the bright sunshine. The opening of their shell is also covered with a slimy gel that prevents air from escaping.

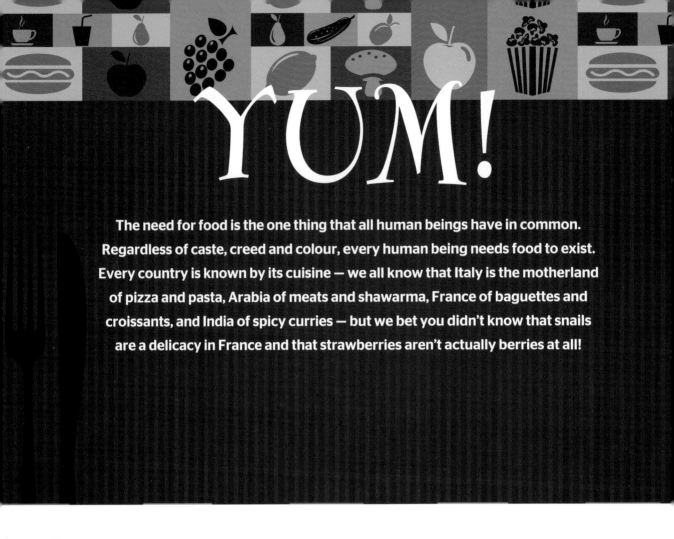

YUM!

The need for food is the one thing that all human beings have in common. Regardless of caste, creed and colour, every human being needs food to exist. Every country is known by its cuisine — we all know that Italy is the motherland of pizza and pasta, Arabia of meats and shawarma, France of baguettes and croissants, and India of spicy curries — but we bet you didn't know that snails are a delicacy in France and that strawberries aren't actually berries at all!

217 Carrots were not always orange in colour.

There was a time when carrots were naturally purple in colour. They were also bitter and not very fleshy, and people rarely ate them. They were grown for their aromatic leaves. The sweet, fleshy, orange carrots that we see everywhere today were first cultivated by Dutch farmers in the late 17th century. The modern carrot is said to have originated in Iran and Afghanistan around 5,000 years ago. This carrot was introduced to Europe via Spain in the 14th century. Orange carrots were then introduced to the rest of the world, including India and America, when the British began colonising these countries.

218 A "baker's dozen" is 13, not 12!

During the 13th century, many ancient societies had extremely strict laws for punishing bakers who cheated their customers. For example, if a baker was caught cheating someone in ancient Egypt, his/her ear would be cut off and nailed to the bakery. Similar punishments were meted out to bakers throughout Europe. Since an accidental miscalculation was always possible, bakers preferred giving a little more than a little less. Therefore, it became a common practice for bakers to give 13 loaves of bread for every dozen that a customer ordered. This ensured that the law was never broken by accident and bakers didn't have to face punishment.

219 Snails are a delicacy in France.

French cuisine is well-known for its high quality, but it is also known for snails! Snails can be prepared in various ways. They are usually served as an appetiser. Sometimes, they are even cooked in sauces and poured over various types of pasta. However, the most popular snail dish is Escargot. To prepare this dish, snails are purged and removed from their shells, and cooked with ingredients such as garlic, butter, chilies, thyme, parsley and nuts. The cooked snails are then placed back into the shells with the butter and sauce before being served. Special snail tongs to hold the shell and snail forks to extract the meat are also provided with the meal. The dish is also popular in Spain.

220 Food can be tasted only if it is mixed with saliva.

Our saliva contains an enzyme known as amylase. This enzyme acts on sugars and other carbohydrates, enabling us to taste. Without saliva, food would not taste the same. We have different receptors all over our tongue for different kinds of tastes. These receptors need liquid so that the different flavours we eat can be bound into the molecules of that receptor. Without liquid, we will not be able to taste. Our saliva provides this liquid, making it possible for us to taste the food that we eat.

221 Honey can never get spoilt.

If honey is preserved well inside a glass container for many years and the container is boiled in a pot of water for a couple of minutes, the honey inside would seem as if it were freshly harvested. Edible forms of honey have been found in ancient Egyptian tombs. Honey contains sugar. Like many other sugars, it doesn't contain much water in its natural state. Bacteria and other kinds of microorganisms that spoil food cannot grow on foods with such low moisture content. Honey is also highly acidic, which kills any bacteria that tries to grow in it.

222 The chemicals in garlic can burn your skin.

Garlic is known to have several medicinal properties. For example, it is used to prevent many kinds of cancer such as rectal cancer, stomach cancer, breast cancer, prostate cancer and bladder cancer.

Garlic has also been used to treat fever, coughs, head and stomach aches, sinus congestion, low blood pressure and snakebites.

But the chemicals in garlic have a number of anti-bacterial and anti-viral properties that can damage human cells. Some of these chemicals can burn your skin if you place a pod of garlic on it. Garlic has allergens and irritants that can cause contact dermatitis or garlic burns.

In addition to inducing severe allergic reactions, if garlic remains in contact with the skin for a long time, it can also cause second or third-degree burns.

Three military soldiers once crushed garlic and rubbed its juice all over their bare arms and legs. They applied the garlic so that they would be relieved from their military duties.

223 In Japan, one of the most popular toppings at Domino's Pizza is squid.

Cheese and pepperoni are the most popular pizza toppings in the world. However, in many places, seafood pizzas are quite common. In Japan, the squid and eel pizzas are popular, while in Russia, people like to eat pizzas that have herring, mackerel, salmon, sardines, tuna and onions. In Australia, shrimp and pineapple toppings are quite popular.

Seafood pizza toppings are a speciality in Asian countries, especially in Eastern Asia. This is because seafood plays an important part in Asian cuisine.

224 Fast food restaurants use colours that stimulate hunger.

Colours are known to evoke emotions in humans. While some colours make us hungry, there are some colours that can curb our appetite. The colour red can attract attention. When we see restaurants that use red, we crave food and we are attracted to the restaurant. On the other hand, when we see the colour yellow, our brain releases a chemical that makes us feel positive and optimistic. This feeling makes us want to eat a large and hearty meal. The colour orange makes us impulsive and excited, encouraging us to eat. These feelings occur at a subconscious level.

225 The first fruit eaten on the moon was a peach.

Man first landed on the moon in 1969. Astronauts Neil Armstrong and Edwin Aldrin were the first men to step on the surface of the moon. Once they landed there, the first fruit they had was the peach. The first ever meal that was eaten on the moon included sugar cookie cubes and bacon squares. During man's early visits to the moon, the food items they carried were dried, so that they contained no moisture. This helped to preserve the food in lightweight, airtight packaging. By doing this, astronauts retained the nutrition and taste of the food items, enabling them to enjoy a balanced meal.

226 Baskin Robbins once made ketchup-flavoured ice cream.

Baskin Robbins often experimented and produced several different kinds of ice cream flavours. Most of these flavours were not sold to the customers. The ketchup ice cream was one such experimental creation. It was the only vegetable flavoured ice cream to be produced. The owners of Baskin Robbins felt that a ketchup flavoured ice cream would not be a popular choice for their customers. So, they stopped making the ice cream.

227 The Snickers candy bar was named after a horse.

The Snickers bar was created by Frank Mars. He was the founder of Mars Inc., that produced other popular candies like Mars bars, Skittles, Dove Chocolate, M&Ms, Milky Way, Twix and other products like Whiskas cat food.

Snickers was the second candy bar sold by Mars Inc., the first being Milky Way. Frank Mars wanted to create a candy bar made of chocolate, to which he added nougat, peanut and caramel. This chocolate bar became quite popular and before long, the sales of the chocolate bar rose quickly.

Mars' wife, Ethel, had a favourite horse called "Snickers" , who passed away just two months before the chocolate bar was launched. In honour of this beloved horse, Mars decided to name his creation after it.

Today, Snickers is the most frequently sold candy bar in the world. It is sold in more than 70 countries and has an annual global sale of over $2 billion.

Snickers is the only chocolate bar in the world that has developed a salad of its own.
The Snickers salad includes a mix of Snickers bars, Granny Smith apples, whipped cream and pudding.

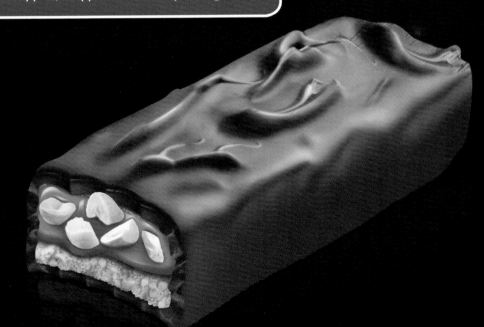

228 Apples are better at waking you up than coffee.

Many people drink coffee to stay awake. The caffeine in coffee is an energy booster that helps people stay alert and active. However, large amounts of caffeine can be harmful to the body. There are many alternatives to coffee that are more effective and healthier than coffee. Apples contain a natural sugar called fructose. Fructose provides energy and helps us stay awake. Additionally, a single apple contains approximately 14 g of carbohydrates, which is used as fuel by our body. The high fibre content in apples helps us stay awake better and longer than a cup of coffee.

229 Cucumbers give you gas.

Cucumbers may make you burp, release gas or give you a stomach ache. They have a high amount of fibre, which helps the body to create waste. This, in turn, produces gas. Cucumbers also contain a substance called cucurbitacin. This substance is responsible for the bitter taste in cucumbers. Cucurbitacin also causes burps, stomach aches and other forms of indigestion. The cucurbitacin content in cucumbers depends on the climate and soil that the cucumbers are grown in. This is why some cucumbers taste more bitter than others.

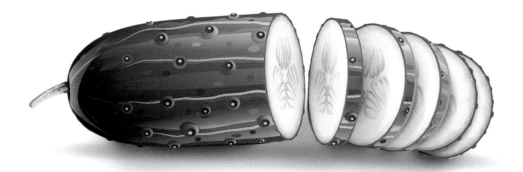

230 Corn flakes were created by accident.

Corn flakes were invented by the Kellogg brothers, who went on to create the Kellogg's company. In 1894, John Kellogg worked as the chief medical officer in the Battle Creek Sanatorium in Michigan, USA. This sanatorium was run on Seventh-day Adventist health principles, which meant that the patients were supposed to follow a vegetarian diet.

William soon developed an interest in health and nutrition, and would regularly help his brother to create new diet plans for the patients. In 1898, the brothers were trying to find a substitute for bread that could be digested easily. This search resulted in them having to boil wheat in order to prepare the dough. The result, however, did not turn into dough. The wheat boiled for a long period and when William tried to roll out the wheat, it separated into flakes. These flakes were quite large and flat. Upon baking these flakes, the Kellogg brothers decided that it would be a good alternative to bread and the flakes came to be called "Granose".

In 1906, William Kellogg prepared the flakes using corn instead of wheat, creating the first corn flakes.

Later, William began adding sugar to his recipes. This created a rift between the brothers as John believed that sugar lowered the health benefits of the cereal.

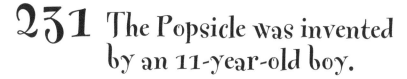

231 The Popsicle was invented by an 11-year-old boy.

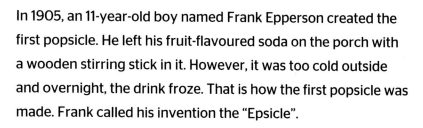

In 1905, an 11-year-old boy named Frank Epperson created the first popsicle. He left his fruit-flavoured soda on the porch with a wooden stirring stick in it. However, it was too cold outside and overnight, the drink froze. That is how the first popsicle was made. Frank called his invention the "Epsicle".

Years later, in 1923, Frank Epperson patented his invention, which was renamed as "popsicle" by his children. In 1925, Epperson sold the popsicle to the Joe Lowe, a company in New York. Back then, popsicle sticks were made from birchwood.

232 Birds' Nest Soup is a delicacy in China.

In China, edible birds' nests have been consumed as food for a long time. When the nest is dissolved in water, it forms a gooey jellylike texture, which can be had as soup.

Birds' nests are also used to prepare other dishes. They are boiled with rice or added to egg tarts. In restaurants, the nests are cooked in chicken broth and served to customers. Soup made from the Asian swift's nest is a highly exquisite delicacy in China. Unlike other birds, the swift prepares its nest with strands of its saliva. These nests are located in dark caves and are generally quite difficult and dangerous to find.

233 The most expensive coffee in the world comes from poop.

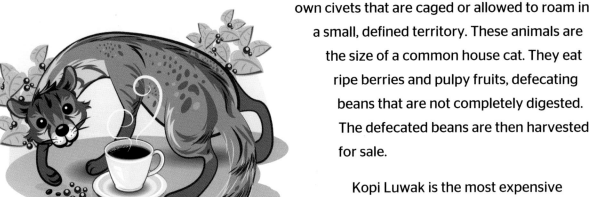

The Kopi Luwak coffee beans come from the excreta of a mammal known as civet. In many places, people own civets that are caged or allowed to roam in a small, defined territory. These animals are the size of a common house cat. They eat ripe berries and pulpy fruits, defecating beans that are not completely digested. The defecated beans are then harvested for sale.

Kopi Luwak is the most expensive coffee in the world, produced mainly on the islands of Sumatra, Java, Bali and Sulawesi, and sold mainly in Japan and USA.

234 The hottest chilli pepper in the world is over 100 times hotter than the jalapeno.

The hottest chilli in the world is the Carolina Reaper. This pepper is said to be a cross between a Pakistani Naga and a Red Habanero. It is cultivated by the PuckerButt Pepper Company in the USA. The level of pungency in a chilli is measured by the Scoville Scale in "Scoville Heat Units" (SHU). While a regular jalapeno pepper would measure anywhere between 1,000-4,000 SHU, the Carolina Reaper is a whopping 15,69,300! Can you imagine how spicy this chilli would be?

235 Lachanophobia is the fear of vegetables.

The word "lachanophobia" is created by merging the Greek words "lachno" meaning "vegetable" and "phobia" meaning "fear". People with this phobia are anxious about vegetables for several reasons.

The primary reason behind this phobia is the fear that the ground on which the vegetables have grown might be contaminated. The phobia can be acquired genetically or due to certain external events that occur at an early age.

The fear of vegetables sounds amusing, but it is a serious matter. People suffering from lachanophobia display a wide range of symptoms on consumption of vegetables, such as fast breathing, irregular heartbeat, dry mouth, gasping for breath, nausea, sweating, stuttering or a feeling of dread. The symptoms may vary, depending on the level of fear in the person.

There are other forms of lachanophobia. For example, lachanophobia mycosis is the fear of mushrooms and lachanophobia lycopersicum is the fear of tomatoes.

236 The first potato chips were meant as an insult.

There was a restaurant called Moon's Lake House near Saratoga Springs in New York. A man named George Crum worked as a chef at this restaurant. Crum enjoyed cooking and could prepare a grand meal out of anything that was edible. He was an incredible chef and the creator of the first potato chips.

In 1853, a guest at Moon's Lake House ordered fried potatoes. Crum made a delicious batch and sent it over to the guest. However, the guest complained that the potatoes were too thick, too soggy and too bland, and asked for another plate.

Crum was so irritated by the cranky guest that he sliced the potatoes paper-thin, fried them longer and added a lot of salt to the dish. Crum was under the impression that the grouchy guest would hate the dish, but his trick wasn't successful. The potato chips went down well with the guest and he ordered for another plate. These were the first potato chips to be created.

It didn't take long for potato chips to grow popular. Crum became a renowned chef and later opened his own restaurant called Crum's House, which served these potato chips. Today, potato chips are a major part of the snack food market in many countries.

The first potato chips were called "Saratoga Chips" as the restaurant where they originated was located near Saratoga Springs.

237 Tarantula legs are a delicacy in Cambodia.

In the town of Skuon in Kampuchea, deep-fried tarantula legs are a popular dish. The dish gained popularity during the food shortage crisis under the rule of the brutal leader, Khmer Rouge. Even after his reign, the dish stuck around and is still enjoyed by Cambodians.

The palm-sized tarantulas are fried in oil, making the dish crispy on the outside and gooey on the inside. The delicacy is called "A-ping" and is seasoned with various spices. The dish may appear disgusting to most people, but is highly nutritious due to its rich protein content.

238 Apples, onions and potatoes have the same taste.

If you were to eat an apple, onion and potato with your nose plugged, they would all taste the same.

This is because your nose plays an important role in the sense of taste. As an apple, onion and potato have the same consistency, you cannot differentiate between their tastes without the sense of smell.

239 Celery contains little to no calories.

Celery is often called a negative calorie food. This means that it requires more energy to digest than what it actually contains. It is exceedingly low in calories. One large stalk contains just six calories.

Celery, like other plants, stores calories in its body. However, as humans, we cannot sufficiently process those calories. The energy stored in celery does not process as it passes through our digestive system. While the stalk contains barely six calories, it takes more than that to digest the entire stalk!

240 Eggs that float on water are bad.

Eggs seem to have a solid shell. However, in reality, these shells are porous. This means that there are very small gaps in the shell, which makes it possible for liquid or air to pass inside.

Once the eggs start aging, more air enters inside through the porous shell. Thus the air cell in the egg grows larger, making it float on water. Fresh eggs, on the other hand, will sink to the bottom if they were placed in a bowl of water.

241 The chocolate chip cookie was invented as an improvement to a butterscotch cookie recipe.

Ruth Graves Wakefield has been credited with the invention of the chocolate chip cookie. She was a dietician as well as lecturer on food, until she began cooking at the inn she and her husband bought, called the Toll House Inn. One of her best recipes was the Butter Drop Do cookies, which was prepared using baker's chocolate.

In 1930, while she was preparing thin butterscotch nut cookies with ice cream, Wakefield decided to improve upon the recipe. So, she took a bar of Nestlé's semi-sweet chocolate and cut it into very small pieces. However, when she baked the cookies, the chocolate did not melt completely; the pieces only softened slightly. This was the first chocolate chip cookie.

Wakefield called her new cookies "Chocolate Crispy Cookies". The guests at the inn loved the cookies and in no time, the cookies became highly popular all over New England. At the same time, the sales of Nestlé's semi-sweet chocolate bar also boomed.

Nestlé struck a deal with Wakefield and agreed to give her a lifetime's supply of chocolate in return for her recipe. The recipe was then printed on every semi-sweet chocolate bar Nestlé produced.

242 Strawberries were used as a medicinal herb.

During the 13th century, strawberries were used as medicinal herbs in France in order to help with problems of indigestion. The fruit, as well as its leaves and roots, worked as a digestive aid. While the fruit was used as a cure to diarrhoea and indigestion, the leaves and roots of the berry helped relieve gout.

Strawberries were also used as a skin tonic. The French rubbed the berries on their sunburnt skins in order to get rid of abnormal marks or blemishes. Strawberries also helped to brighten teeth and get rid of bad breath.

243 Chewing gum while peeling onions can keep you from crying.

Did you know that when we cry, tears do not come from our eyes? They are actually produced by small glands (called lachrymal glands) located in the corners of our eyes. These glands produce tears when they are irritated.

Onions release a chemical called syn-propanethial-S-oxide into the air when they are cut. This chemical irritates the lachrymal glands, thus resulting in tears. When we chew gum, we tend to breathe through our mouths. The irritant gets dissolved and a smaller amount of the chemical reaches the lachrymal glands. This way, the glands cannot produce tears and we do not cry.

244 Ancient Mayans made hot chocolate with chillies and corn.

The first records of chocolate being used as a drink date back to the 5th century CE. A residue of the chocolate drink made by the Mayan civilisation in South America was found in an ancient pot.

The Mayans had a unique way of preparing their chocolate drink. They crushed beans of chocolate into a fine powder and added water to prepare a chocolate paste. A number of assorted spices such as chillies, peppers as well as cornmeal were added to the paste.

245 Pretzels were invented by a monk.

Around 610 CE, a German monk wanted to make something useful with the pieces of dough left over from baking bread. He took the pieces, rolled them into thin strips and folded them into a looped twist. This was the first pretzel.

The monks would teach prayers to little children. If the children learned and recited their prayers well, they were given a pretzel as a treat. The looped twist in the pretzel represents the arms of the children folded in prayer. The pretzels were then called "pretiola", which is Latin for "little reward".

246 Chicken tikka masala originated in the UK.

Chicken tikka masala, a popular Indian dish, was first made in Glasgow. It was created by accident in the Shish Mahal restaurant in Glasgow, when a guest wanted some curry to go with his chicken. The chef, a Pakistani man named Ali Ahmed Aslam, prepared a sauce by cooking yoghurt, cream and an assortment of spices together. This was the first chicken tikka masala to be prepared.

Approximately one among seven curries sold in Britain are tikka masala. The dish is also highly popular in most restaurants in India.

247 Pearls melt in vinegar.

There is a legend that says how Cleopatra, the ruler of Egypt, melted her pearls in a vessel containing vinegar. Cleopatra was the owner of two large pearls that were passed down to her through the hands of the Kings of the East. She wore the pearls as earrings. When the vinegar container was placed before her, she took off one earring and dropped it in the vinegar. The vinegar completely melted the pearl and it is believed that Cleopatra swallowed the mixture later.

MONUMENTAL MARVELS

Since ancient times, man has created several magnificent monuments that have filled the world with awe. Whether these monuments have been created to honour a person or as a reminder of a significant event, they have gone down in history as the marvels of architecture.

248 The entire city of Machu Picchu was built without the use of wheels or animals.

Machu Picchu is an ancient city in South America. It was built by the Inca civilisation, 8,000 ft above sea level. It is located on a ridge between the Huayna Picchu and Machu Picchu mountains in Peru. The Incas did not use any animals or tools to build the city. Instead, they polished quarried granite stone themselves and fitted them together tightly. This building technique prevented any major damage to the structures, even during earthquakes.

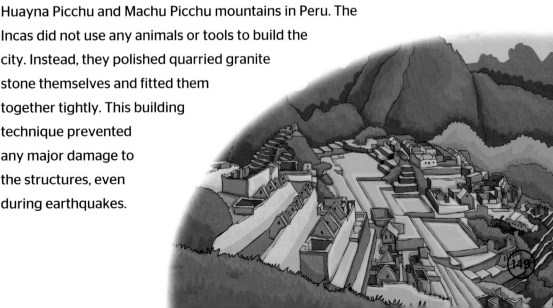

249 The desert city of Petra had a water system that could support the entire city.

Petra is a city in the country of Jordan in Western Asia. The city was once highly prosperous and an important junction of the silk trade in the continent.

Today, the city of Petra is one of the wonders of the world. Petra is famous for its unique architecture and excellent water conduit system. There was enough water in Petra to satisfy the 30,000 people that lived there and even more to have lush gardens in the desert region.

250 Some of the stones of the Stonehenge were dragged 150 miles to the site.

The Stonehenge, a collection of gigantic stones, is a monument in England. It was built in 2600 BCE. The stones in the Stonehenge were not situated at the site, but in Wales. From there, they were dragged all way to England, a distance of almost 150 miles, and put in a specific formation. There are almost 900 such stone structures all over Britain. The Stonehenge is the biggest of them all. The biggest stone in the monument is over 22 ft in height and weighs up to 40 tonnes!

251 The Great Pyramid of Giza points very precisely to the north.

The pyramids of Egypt are the most incredible man-made structures in history. They are one of the oldest monuments in the world and have been preserved quite well. Every year, millions of people go all way to Egypt to see these magnificent structures.

The pyramids were built as tombs for the Pharaohs of Egypt. They were massive in size as the Pharaohs were buried with many of their personal items and treasures. The biggest pyramid of all is the Great Pyramid of Giza. It is the only surviving wonder of the Seven Wonders of the Ancient World. The structure is almost 480 ft tall and took over 20 years to complete.

The architecture of this pyramid was planned with great precision. The base was a perfect square and the top pointed to the north. Ancient Egyptians had learnt about the value of pi, so they designed the angle of the pyramid to be precisely 51°, 51 minutes and 14.3 seconds.

> The pyramids of Egypt were built on the western side of the Nile River that flows through the country. This area then came to be known as "the land of the dead".

252 The top of the Eiffel Tower sways during strong winds.

The Eiffel Tower is a gigantic tower situated in Paris, France. It was the tallest structure in the world when it was built in 1889. Its height today is 1,063 ft. That's almost the height of an 81-storied building! You need to climb 1,665 steps to reach the top. That's a lot!

There are four pillars at the base on which the tower stands. It tapers towards the top. The tower was built to be resistant to wind. However, if the wind is too strong, the top sways almost up to 7 cm.

253 The Empire State Building has its own zip code.

The Empire State Building is a building in New York, USA. The 1,454 ft building took just a year and 45 days to build, unlike other monuments that take years to complete. There is also a basement in the building that goes 35 ft below the ground.

Offices of several companies are based in the 102-storied commercial complex. Due to a large number of offices in the building, it has its own zip code.

254 The Colosseum in Rome had 76 entrances and exits.

The Colosseum is a huge amphitheatre in Italy. It was built a long time ago by the slaves of the Roman Empire. Roman slaves, who were called gladiators, would fight each other to death in the arena, while citizens and other nobles watched with amusement from the stands.

When the Colosseum was built, it was the largest amphitheatre in the Empire. 50,000 people could be accommodated in the theatre, which covered almost six acres of land. The Colosseum had four levels, each level occupied by people of the same social status. It also had several underground passages as well as 32 trapdoors underneath its mighty frame.

There were 76 entrances and exits in the entire monument. This was to help people evacuate the theatre quickly in case of emergencies such as fires.

One of the exits in the western section of the amphitheatre was known as the "Gate of Death". It was called so because the gladiators who died in the arena were carried out of this exit.

255 The Big Ben chimes every 15 minutes.

The Big Ben is a clock tower in England. The largest bell in the tower was given the nickname, which came to be associated with the entire monument.

In addition to the great bell are four quarter bells that play to the melody of Westminster Quarters every 15 minutes. The number of chime sets matches the number of quarter hours that pass. The sound of the massive monument can be heard for a radius of up to 8 km.

256 The seven spikes on the Statue of Liberty's crown represent the seven continents.

The Statue of Liberty in the USA is the universal symbol of freedom. The torch in the right hand of the statue stands for liberty while the tablet in the left hand is the Declaration of Independence.

The seven spikes on the crown refer to the people of the seven continents that the Lady of Liberty is addressing, i.e., North America, South America, Europe, Africa, Asia, Australia and Antarctica. The chains that lie at the feet are the shackles of tyranny that the Lady has escaped from.

257 The monument of Hagia Sophia has been a church as well as a mosque.

Hagia Sophia is a monument in Constantinople (now Istanbul), Turkey, a country located in the far west of Asia. The monument was built under the direction of Byzantine emperor Justinian I in the 6th century CE on the site of a church that was destroyed in a fire. This destroyed church was originally built by Constantine in 537 CE. Justinian wanted to build the largest church in the world. It took six years to build this grand structure.

In 1453, Constantinople was seized by the Turkish Empire. The Ottoman Turks began to convert all the churches in the city into mosques. The Hagia Sophia was also converted to a mosque by adding a chandelier and disks with Islamic calligraphy, among other additions. Four minarets were built on the corners of the dome, which is a classic style of Islamic architecture. The crescent was also placed on the top of the dome. Hagia Sophia was then renamed as "Ayasofya Camii".

The monument remained a mosque for almost five centuries before the first President of Turkey, Mustafa Kemal Atatürk, converted the mosque into a museum in 1935. Hagia Sophia exists as a museum even today.

There are 40 windows in the Hagia Sophia. The light that comes in through the windows casts fantastic shadows, giving the monument a magical look.

258 Michelangelo's statue of David was carved from a single chunk of marble.

The statue of David in the city of Florence, Italy, was made by Italian sculptor Michelangelo sometime between 1501 and 1504.

When Michelangelo came to Florence, he was granted a commission to make a huge statue of the Biblical hero David. He was given a single enormous chunk of marble to create the sculpture. He spent several days and nights in secrecy and would not let anyone see the statue until it was finished. The result turned out to be one of Michelangelo's most famous works of art.

259 None of the paintings inside St. Peter's Basilica are actually paintings.

St. Peter's Basilica is a church in Vatican City. The paintings in the church cover 10,000 m² of wall. But they aren't really paintings. The images covering the walls of the church are, in reality, mosaics. The paintings that once existed in the church were ruined because of humidity and mould, and had to be replaced by mosaics. The mosaics have been created in such great detail, they appear similar to the original paintings.

260 The Washington Monument was supposed to be a pantheon.

George Washington was the first President of the USA. When he died, the Continental Congress of America wanted to commemorate his death by building a monument. A design competition was held and winner's design was to be used as the principal design.

Robert Mills designed a pantheon, with the statue of Washington above the main entrance. While this design won the competition, the project was put on hold due to a shortage of funds and resumed several decades later. By then, architectural tastes had changed and the plan to have a pantheon was scrapped.

261 Over 90% of Mount Rushmore was carved using dynamite.

The Mount Rushmore National Memorial depicts the heads of four US presidents—George Washington, Thomas Jefferson, Theodore Roosevelt and Abraham Lincoln. The faces on the mountain are 60 ft high. It took 14 years to build and required around 350 people!

To create this, the builders used dynamite. They would cut and set charges of precise dynamite sizes. The finishing touches were done using air hammers.

262 The White House requires over 2000 l of paint to cover its outside surface.

The White House in the USA is an enormous palace where the president of the country lives. It has 132 rooms, 32 bathrooms and 6 levels to provide accommodations for all the people who live and work there. The entire structure is 168 ft long, 152 ft wide and almost 70 ft in height.

Such a large building will obviously require a great amount of paint. It is estimated that approximately 2,150 l of "Whisper White" paint are required just to paint the exterior. The white paint is what gives the building its name.

263 The Sydney Opera House has more than 10,000 pipes.

The Sydney Opera House is a performing arts centre in Sydney, Australia. The entire structure has five theatres. The Opera House regularly hosts a number of events, including music concerts, circus performances, plays and stand-up comedy, and can accommodate more than 2,600 people.

A striking feature of the concert hall is the Sydney Opera House Grand Organ. It is the largest pipe organ in the world and it consists of 10,154 pipes!

264 Michelangelo painted the ceiling of the Sistine Chapel while lying on his back.

The Sistine Chapel is a chapel of the Apostolic Palace, where the Pope lives. Situated in Vatican City, the chapel was built sometime between 1473 and 1483. The most striking feature of this chapel is its ceiling, featuring several paintings.

The ceiling of the Sistine Chapel was painted by many famous artists such as Michelangelo and Botticelli. Michelangelo had repainted the ceiling upon the request of the Pope in 1508. Michelangelo spent four years completing the paintings by lying on his back for several hours a day. The result turned out to be a masterpiece. The paintings depicted scenes from the Bible, the holy book of Christians.

265 The Tower Bridge was chocolate brown in colour.

The Tower Bridge is a bridge in London across the River Thames. The bridge was built in 1894 in the East End of London. It was 800 ft long and had two towers built on piers.

In 1894, the Tower Bridge was painted chocolate brown in colour and it remained that way until 1977, when it was repainted red, white and blue, the colours of the British National Flag.

266 The Parthenon once held a Turkish mosque.

The Parthenon in Athens, Greece, is a shrine dedicated to Athena, a mythological goddess of the Greeks. The Parthenon is situated on top of a hill in the centre of the city of Athens, which derives its name from the goddess.

In 1458, the Ottoman Turks invaded Athens. As per their custom, they turned the shrine of Parthenon into a mosque. However, they did not make too many changes in the structure. Two centuries later, the monument was destroyed in an explosion. Today, only ruins of the ancient shrine remain.

267 The Golden Gate Bridge is actually a toll bridge.

The Golden Gate Bridge of San Francisco is quite popular. It has appeared in several Hollywood movies and even on the cover of the Rolling Stone Magazine. The bridge is a 2,737 m long channel between San Francisco Bay and the Pacific Ocean. Every year, about 41 million cars cross the Golden Gate Bridge.

Today, the Golden Gate Bridge is one of the most internationally recognised symbols of San Francisco. However, many people do not know that the bridge is actually a toll bridge. Every vehicle has to pay a toll of $7 to cross the bridge.

268 The longest man-made structure in the world is the Great Wall of China.

The Great Wall of China covers most of the northern region of the country. As China is the fourth-largest country in the world, you can imagine how long the Great Wall is. It stretches for almost 8851 km!

In 700 BCE, China was facing regular attacks from the Mongols. To keep the Mongols out, Chinese rulers started building walls in their states. Several walls were constructed in the northern regions of China. In 221 BCE, Chinese Emperor Qin Shi Huang ordered for all the walls to be joined together. That's how the Great Wall of China came to be built. It is almost 33 ft high and 15 ft wide.

Imagine how difficult it must have been to build such a mighty wall! Millions of people were involved in the construction, which went on for 1,000 years. The people building the monument were peasants, slaves or criminals, all of whom were not paid for their efforts. Most of them died during the construction and were buried under the wall.

In the 14th century, the Great Wall was rebuilt by the Ming Dynasty of China. The wall was earlier built of earth and stone. The new wall was much stronger as it was built from bricks. This is the wall that we see today.

269 The first person to be buried in St. Paul's cathedral was its designer.

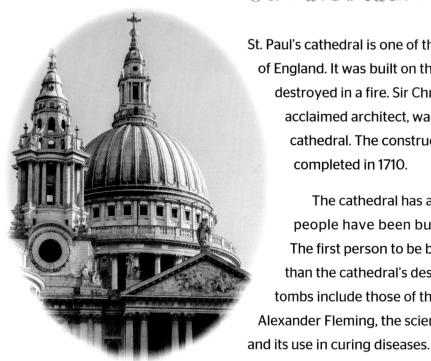

St. Paul's cathedral is one of the most remarkable structures of England. It was built on the site of a church that was destroyed in a fire. Sir Christopher Wren, a highly acclaimed architect, was the chief designer of the cathedral. The construction of the cathedral was completed in 1710.

The cathedral has a crypt where several famous people have been buried over the years. The first person to be buried there was none other than the cathedral's designer himself. Other noteworthy tombs include those of the Duke of Wellington and Alexander Fleming, the scientist who discovered penicillin and its use in curing diseases.

270 The Notre Dame Cathedral was saved by a novel.

The Notre Dame was a monument in Paris that went through severe damages during the French Revolution. However, there were no efforts towards its restoration or protection.

In 1831, Victor Hugo published a novel called *The Hunchback of Notre Dame*, which was based on this monument. This novel stirred emotions among the French, which made them realise that they must preserve the magnificent cathedral. Restoration work began in 1845 and the monument stands tall even today.

271 The statue of Christ the Redeemer was made in France.

Christ the Redeemer, or "Cristo Redentor", as it is colloquially called, is one of the most famous monuments in Rio de Janeiro, Brazil. The construction of the statue was completed in 1931.

The statue is 98 ft tall and its arms are 92 ft wide. It is the symbol of Christianity all over the world and the icon of Brazil. However, the construction of the statue did not take place in Brazil. It happened in France. The statue was transported to Rio de Janeiro in tiny pieces. The head of the statue alone was made up of 50 individual parts. The pieces were then put together in Rio de Janeiro to complete the structure.

The statue of Christ with his arms wide apart signifies that God loves everyone and will embrace all who come to God. The statue resembles a cross from a distance.

272 The largest religious monument in the world is the Angkor Wat.

Man has been building places of worship since ancient times. The largest religious structure in the world is the Angkor Wat in Kampuchea, Cambodia. The Angkor Wat was built by King Suryavarman II as an administrative centre for his empire. The entire complex stretches up to 24 km from east to west and 13 km north to south. The temples in Angkor Wat are devoted to the Hindu god Vishnu. The temple derives its name from "Angkor", meaning "city" and "Wat" meaning "monastery".

273 The Atomium Building was not intended to survive beyond the 1958 Brussels World's Fair.

The Atomium is a building in Brussels, Belgium, known for its distinctive architecture. The building consists of nine spheres connected together, resembling the iron molecule. This unique architecture was constructed for the Brussels World Fair in 1958. But the building grew very popular and the plans to demolish it were cancelled.

The Atomium Building is 102 m tall. Tubes connect the nine spheres, that have escalators and an elevator. The elevator, which accommodates 22 people, can get you to the top sphere in 23 seconds.

274 The Brandenburg Gate was once a symbol for fascist Germany.

The Brandenburg Gate is a popular tourist attraction in Germany. It was built as a sign of peace after a long period of war in 1791. However, when Hitler rose to power, the Brandenburg Gate became a symbol of the Nazi party. During the Cold War, the Berlin Wall divided Germany into two halves. The wall ran round the back of the Brandenburg Gate. When the wall was breached in 1989, the Brandenburg Gate once again became a symbol of unity.

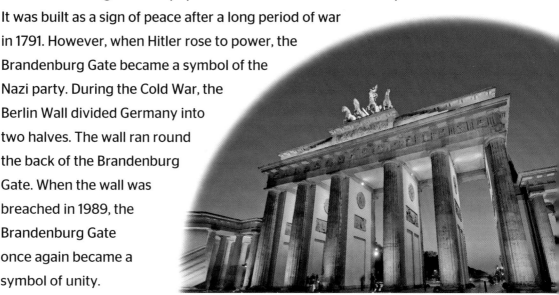

275 Edward Jones broke into the Buckingham Palace thrice.

The royal family of Britain has been residing in the Buckingham Palace since 1837. It has more than 775 rooms, which includes 19 state rooms, 52 royal and guest bedrooms, 188 staff bedrooms, 92 offices, 78 bathrooms and a cinema.

Between 1838 and 1841, a young boy, Edward Jones, broke into the palace thrice. He was called "the boy Jones" and is the world's first celebrity stalker! He was obsessed with Queen Victoria and was caught stealing her underwear when he was just 14.

276 The Pantheon is a pagan temple transformed into a church.

Christianity was a minority religion in the Roman Empire during the 4th century. In 312 CE, Maxentius seized the Roman throne and declared war on Constantine, who also desired the throne. Maxentius was a pagan who hated Christians. Constantine took advantage of his hatred and converted to Christianity. Once Constantine rose to power, he legalised the religion of Christianity and began persecuting every pagan cult. Several temples were destroyed and rebuilt as churches in the process. The Pantheon in Rome, which was a temple of ancient Roman deities, was turned into a Roman Catholic Church dedicated to St. Mary and the Martyrs.

277 The Golden Temple has four entrances in the North, East, South and West.

The Golden Temple in Amritsar, India, is the most sacred place of worship for the Sikhs. Though it is a temple chiefly for the Sikhs, it is open to people of all religions. There are four entrances to the temple, one in each direction. The four entrances indicate that people from all four corners of Earth are welcome.

Equality to all is the principle of Sikhism. Every day, the Golden Temple provides free meals for 35,000 people. The food is sponsored by temple volunteers. Everyone who eats at the temple has to sit on the floor, irrespective of caste, status or wealth.

278 The El Castillo at Chichen Itza has 365 steps, representing each day of the year.

Chichen Itza is an ancient city in Mexico. It was built by the people of the ancient Mayan civilisation. The city was flourishing from 800 to 1200 CE. However, the structures that were built in the city exist even today.

The significant features of this city include a stepped pyramid, various temples, an observatory and a ball court.

The El Castillo, one of the most remarkable structures of the city, is a temple in the shape of a stepped pyramid. The Mayans were skilled in the science of astronomy, which is evident from the structure of the pyramid. It has 365 steps, representing the 365 days of the year. The Mayans had thus built the first ever calendar. On every first day of the seasons of spring and fall, the Sun would cast a shadow on the steps of the pyramid. The shadow looked like a snake trying to wiggle its way down the pyramid.

The Mayans' knowledge and expertise in astronomy is also reflected in other structures found at Chichen Itza, such as the observatory of El Caracol. The Mayans used the tower of the observatory to study stars and predict eclipses.

279 The highest palace in the world is the Potala Palace in Tibet.

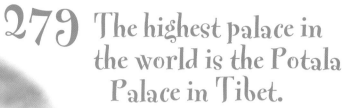

During the 20th century, there was a constant conflict between China and Tibet. The uprising ended with China taking control of Tibet and the Dalai Lama escaping to India. The Potala Palace in Lhasa, Tibet, was the chief residence of the Dalai Lama before the uprising. The palace is situated on the Red Hill of Lhasa and is the highest palace in the world, at an altitude of 3,650 m above sea level.

280 Each head at Madame Tussauds wax museum takes five weeks to make.

Madame Tussauds is the most well-known wax museum in the world. Located in London, it houses around 400 wax statues!

The museum is known for its life-like statues. In fact, a device even makes Sleeping Beauty's chest heave as she sleeps! The hair used on the head, moustaches and beards are real—which means that each one has to be inserted individually. This means that each head takes approximately five weeks to make. As the hair on the statues is real, all the statues' hair is regularly shampooed and their clothes are regularly laundered.

281 Emperor Shah Jahan ordered the hands of his workers to be chopped off after building the Taj Mahal.

The Taj Mahal is a monument in India that was built by a Mughal Emperor, Shah Jahan, for his wife. When Emperor Shah Jahan's wife, Mumtaz Mahal, died, he was very upset and built this beautiful mausoleum in her honour.

The walls of the Taj Mahal are made of pure white marble. They also hold a number of precious gems and stones. However, the grandest feature of the mausoleum is Mumtaz Mahal's tomb. It is adorned with a number of stones, including the lapis lazuli, which was ordered from the neighbouring country of Afghanistan, sapphires brought from Sri Lanka and jasper from the Indian state of Punjab.

When the construction of Taj Mahal was complete, it was the most remarkable structure in the region. Shah Jahan was afraid that the artists and builders would recreate the marvellous monument. To avoid that, he ordered the hands of all the workers to be chopped off.

In spite of Shah Jahan's efforts, several replicas of the Taj Mahal were made. The Bibi Ka Maqbara was a replica made by Shah Jahan's son Aurangzeb.

282 The Tower of Pisa is tilted.

The most remarkable feature of the Tower of Pisa is that it leans in one direction. The tower is known all over the world as the Leaning Tower of Pisa.

As the name suggests, the tower is located in Pisa, Italy. The city derived its name from a Greek word meaning "marshy land". The soil in Pisa is too marshy to support tall structures. In addition, there are layers of sand and clay in the soil. The weight of the mighty tower compressed the layers of soil beneath it. Given how unstable the soil is, the tower sunk deeper in certain places. This made the tower tilt.

The construction of the tower took a long time. After building the foundation and the first few floors, construction was stopped for some years because of a war. During this time, the soil under the tower had settled, strengthening the formation. The complete construction of the tower was done in three stages. If the gaps in construction hadn't occurred, the tower would have collapsed. A number of restoration works have also helped to strengthen the monument.

There are seven bells on the topmost floor of the Tower of Pisa. Each bell represents a note of the musical major scale.

283 The CN Tower is the world's tallest lightning rod.

The CN Tower in Canada is a popular tourist attraction and a pride for Canadians in Toronto, where it is located. The tower is 1,815 ft high, including a 335-ft antenna that is placed on top of the tower to absorb lightning.

Lightning strikes the tower more than 75 times a year. There are copper strips that run down the tower to the grounding rods that are buried below the ground. In this way, the lightning is transported to the ground without hurting anyone. You can be safe even if you are inside the building when lightning strikes.

284 The Turning Torso Building is modelled on the human body.

The Turning Torso in Sweden is a skyscraper based on a sculpture called Twisting Torso, which is a twisted human being. Situated in Sweden, the Turning Torso is the tallest building in all of Scandinavia.

The skyscraper is 190 m high and has a 90° twist. The structure consists of nine cubes with five floors on each cube. The 54-storied building houses residences as well as offices. The building also has its own wine cellar, where the tenants can store their wine.

285 If laid end to end, the Burj Khalifa can stretch over a quarter of the world.

The Burj Khalifa is the tallest building in the world. Situated in Dubai, the tower is 2,716.5 ft in height. That makes it thrice as tall as the Eiffel Tower and almost twice as tall as the Empire State Building. If the rebar used to construct the building were to be laid down end to end, it would extend over a quarter of the way around the world.

The Burj Khalifa has 163 floors with an observation deck on the 124th floor, a swimming pool on the 76th floor and a restaurant on the 122nd floor. It also houses 900 residences within the building, making it the world's tallest structure to include residential space.

286 The Taipei 101 tower does not have a 44th floor because four is considered unlucky.

Taipei 101 is a skyscraper in Taipei, Taiwan. It was the tallest building in the world before the Burj Khalifa was built. The tower is a symbol of technology and Asian tradition. The name of the tower indicates that the Taipei 101 has 101 floors.

But according to Chinese culture, the number "four" is considered unlucky. So, what ought to be the 44th floor in the Taipei 101 has been replaced by Level 43, with 42A replacing the actual 43!

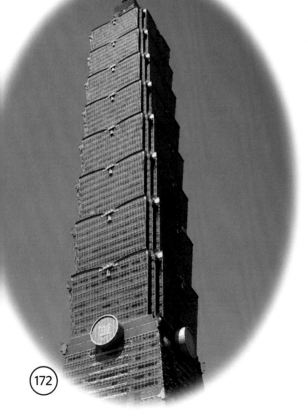

LITERATI

You've heard their names and you've read their books—well, some of them, at least. Authors, especially the great ones, have always had a reputation for being quirky and rather "odd" by normal standards. This means that there's a treasure of unknown facts about them and their works for us to explore!

287 Shakespeare wrote a play and a half in a year.

Shakespeare is one of the best-known playwrights in English literature. His plays captured the complete range of human emotion and conflict. He wrote for an English theatre troupe called "The Lord Chamberlain's Men". His plays were very famous and are read and enjoyed by many even today. He first started writing in 1589. By the time he died in 1616, he had written 37 plays and 154 sonnets—that's an average of one and a half plays a year!

288 John Milton wrote *Paradise Lost* 16 years after he lost his eyesight.

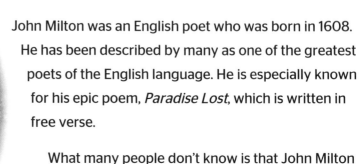

John Milton was an English poet who was born in 1608. He has been described by many as one of the greatest poets of the English language. He is especially known for his epic poem, *Paradise Lost*, which is written in free verse.

What many people don't know is that John Milton had been steadily going blind for years. By 1652, he was completely blind. But Milton didn't let that stop him. He dictated his poetry out loud to a transcriber for as long as he could and asked his daughters to read to him on a daily basis.

289 Daniel Defoe was also a spy.

Daniel Defoe was born in 1660 and was the son of a butcher, James Foe. He was a prolific and versatile writer, writing more than 500 books, journals and pamphlets on several different topics. He was also a journalist and a spy who was thrown into prison for a few days! He was a spy for Robert Harley, Chancellor of the Exchequer, in the year before the Scottish Union. Even after the union in 1707, Defoe continued as a political writer. Today, he is best known for his novel, *Robinson Crusoe*. He was also one of the first people to popularise "novels" in Britain.

290 Charles Dickens made the first ever reference to potato chips.

Charles Dickens is considered to be one of the greatest authors of the Victorian era and even has a verb named after him! Any work written in his style is called "Dickensian". Charles Dickens has been credited with introducing 247 new words or usages to the English language. Some of these include butter-fingers, cheesiness and fluffiness. In his book, *Tale of Two Cities*, he mentions "husky chips of potato, fried with some reluctant drops of oil". This is the earliest reference to potato chips in the world!

A lot of critics have said that Dickens' books are very melancholic and depressing. But this is because of his own difficult childhood. His father was sent to prison because he couldn't pay his debts. Charles had to work in very rough conditions at a shoe polish factory to earn money. Though he didn't have much formal training and was forced to drop out of school, he enjoyed reading and trained himself to be a journalist. His book, *The Pickwick Papers*, was published in monthly installments.

Dickens was known for his humorous and satirical style. He had a fake bookcase with books that were hilariously titled, including *Noah's Arkitechture* and a nine-volume set titled *Cat's Lives*.

291 Victor Hugo put himself under house arrest to write *The Hunchback of Notre-Dame.*

Victor Hugo had an agreement with his publisher to complete the novel in 1829. But due to delays in other projects, he was unable to begin work on it even by 1830. His agitated publisher gave him the deadline of February 1831. Victor Hugo began work on the novel in September 1830, with the seemingly impossible deadline of February 1831 in mind. He bought an entire bottle of ink in preparation and put himself under house arrest for months, using the strangest anti-escaping techniques. He locked away all his clothes and bought a large, grey shawl for the occasion. For the next six months, he wrote at home, wearing just the shawl. Finally, weeks before the deadline, he finished his novel.

The book was written to protest against the breaking down of medieval architecture to make way for "modern buildings". This is perhaps why the novel contains so much description that isn't essential to the plot of the story.

Victor Hugo's famous work *Les Miserables* has a sentence that is 823 words long.

292 Lewis Carroll never meant to publish *Alice in Wonderland.*

Lewis Carroll never meant to be an author. He was a shy child, but he was exceptionally bright. He was extremely good at mathematics and was offered a position as a professor at Christ Church, Oxford. He even published several mathematical publications. He would often entertain the Dean's children by narrating stories that he would make up. One of the Dean's daughters was named Alice. He began telling her a story about a young girl named Alice who chased a rabbit down a hole. He wrote it down for her. Later, a writer named Henry Kingsley found it and convinced him to publish it. The book, *Alice in Wonderland*, is considered a children's classic even today.

293 Sir Arthur Conan Doyle didn't want to be known solely as the creator of Sherlock Holmes.

Sherlock Holmes, the master detective, has featured in numerous films and series. But his creator, Sir Arthur Conan Doyle, was once known to have said, "If in one hundred years I am known only as the man who invented Sherlock Holmes, then I will have considered my life to be a failure." He had a varied career as a writer, journalist and public figure. He even had a degree in medicine. In 1893, he killed off the character of Sherlock Holmes in order to concentrate on more writing, but was forced to bring him back to life on public demand.

294 Leo Tolstoy never completed college.

Leo Tolstoy is a famous Russian author known for his realistic fiction. His best known works are his novels, *War and Peace* and *Anna Karenina*. He was born into Russian nobility on 9th September, 1828. But he was never a good student! In fact, when he enrolled in the Oriental Languages programme at the University of Kazan, he never got good grades. His teachers even described him as, "both unable and unwilling to learn". He left the university after two years and never completed his degree, but he continued teaching himself.

Eventually, he was fluent in at least a dozen languages. He expressed ideas of non-violent resistance in his book, *The Kingdom of God is Within You,* which later influenced people like Gandhi and Martin Luther King Jr.

Leo Tolstoy died at the Astapavo station in Russia. What's rather strange is that Anna Karenina, the lead character in one of his most famous novels, also died at this station!

295 Six people have declined the Nobel Prize in literature.

The Nobel Prize was declined by six people! Two of them voluntarily declined it, while four others were forced to decline it. Boris Pasternak was awarded the prize in 1958. He accepted it but was then forced to decline by his country (Soviet Union). Jean Paul Sartre was then awarded the prize in 1964. He did not accept the prize because he believed that accepting the prize would mean aligning himself with the institution. Adolf Hitler forbade three German Nobel Laureates, Richard Kuhn, Adolf Butenandt and Gerhard Domagk, from accepting the prize. Le Duc Tho declined his 1973 Nobel Peace Prize due to the political situation in Vietnam.

296 Miguel de Cervantes got the idea for *Don Quixote* when in prison.

Don Quixote is a Spanish novel written by Miguel de Cervantes in the 1600s. It was originally published in two volumes in 1605 and 1615. The book is about the misadventures of a man who becomes so absorbed in the tales of knights that he decides to become one himself. He then rides around the Spanish countryside, trying to uplift the downtrodden. It is a satire on chivalry and de Cervantes is said to have got the idea while he was in prison in 1602. With more than 500 million copies sold, some call it the bestselling novel of all time.

297 Mark Twain didn't even complete elementary school.

With more than 28 books to his credit, including *The Adventures of Tom Sawyer* and *The Adventures of Huckleberry Finn*, it's hard to believe that Mark Twain did not even complete elementary school!

Samuel Clemens, later known as Mark Twain, was born on 30th November, 1835, in the small town of Hannibal, Missouri. He was forced to drop out of school after his father's death, when he was just 12. He started working as a printer's apprentice. Two years later, he started writing for his brother's newspaper. It was here that he discovered his passion for writing. When he was 17, he left the printer's job and became a river pilot's apprentice.

He became a licenced river pilot in 1859. "Mark Twain" is a river term which means that it is safe to navigate. He began working as a newspaper reporter during the civil war because the river trade was brought to a standstill.

His rise to fame began when his story, *The Celebrated Jumping Frog of Calavaras County* appeared in the New York Saturday Press. He published his first book, *The Innocents Abroad*, in 1869.

Mark Twain passed away on 21st April, 1910, but has a following even today. His childhood home is open to the public as a museum in Hannibal. The Calavaras County holds the Calavaras County Fair and Jumping Frog Jubilee every third weekend in May in honour of Twain.

298 There's a novel that contains just one sentence.

Dancing Lessons for the Advanced in Age is a Czechoslovakian novel written by Bohumil Hrabal. It narrates the story of a man who is remembering various events from his life, particularly his love life. What's extraordinary about this book is that the entire novel, all 117 pages of it, is told in one long sentence. Many people regard Bohumil Hrabal as the most influential Czech writer. Another similar book is *The Gates of Paradise* by Polish author, Jerzy Andrzejewski. The book is 40,000 words long and contains only two sentences—the second of which is only four words long.

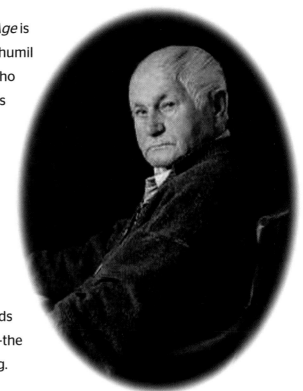

299 The longest sentence in the English language is 13,955 words long.

Inspired by Bohumil Hrabal's *Dancing Lessons for the Advanced in Age*, Jonathan Coe, a British author, wrote a similar book, titled *The Rotter's Club*. The book traces the experiences of three teenage friends as they grow up in Britain in the 1970s. It traces the changes their lives go through as their world gets involved with IRA bombs, progressive and punk rock, girls and political strikes. It has a sentence that is 13,955 words long.

300 Enid Blyton wrote more than 700 books throughout her lifetime.

Enid Blyton is possibly one of the most well-known children's authors of all time. She has written many mystery and adventure series where children are the protagonists with little or no help from adults. Her work has been translated into more than 90 languages. When she was barely 14 years old, she won a poetry competition, which encouraged her to submit stories, articles and poems to magazines. But her poetry wasn't published in the beginning. Her first published work was an article on children and education in a magazine called *Nash Magazine*.

301 Sidney Sheldon didn't start writing novels until he was in his 50s.

Before pursuing a career as an author, Sidney Sheldon made a living by writing TV shows.

In fact, he worked in television for 20 years. He made shows like *The Patty Duke Show* and *I Dream of Jeannie*. He wrote the script for almost every episode of these shows. He started writing books only after he turned 50. He wrote 18 novels, which sold 300 million copies. He even published an autobiography in which he speaks of his struggles with bipolar disorder.

302 Virginia Woolf once dressed up as a Prince and got treated as royalty.

Horace de Vere Cole was an Irish poet, known for his love of practical jokes. In 1910, he plotted a prank that shot him to fame along with five of his friends, one of whom was Virginia Woolf. All five of them applied make-up to make them significantly darker and wore exotic robes and turbans. Cole wrote a telegraph announcing the arrival of dignitaries from Abyssinia, an African country, on board the HMS Dreadnought and signed it off as a government official.

He pretended to be the group's interpreter. They arranged for a VIP carriage to take them to the ship. Since none of the pranksters spoke an African dialect, they used mangled versions of Greek and Latin. Every time they were shown something adequately impressive, they declared "Bunga! Bunga!" They were given a royal treatment and even invited to dine, which they refused, afraid that their make-up and beards may end up in the soup! The group returned to London after an extremely successful prank.

When the Dreadnought sunk an enemy ship in World War I, the navy received one telegram congratulating them by saying, "Bunga! Bunga!"

303 Roald Dahl was a spy before he started writing children's novels.

Roald Dahl is one of the most celebrated children's authors of all time and most of his books have also been turned into movies. But his life was quite exciting and writing children's books was certainly not his only profession. He served in the British Royal Air Force during World War II. His experiences have been recorded in his autobiography, *Going Solo*. However, his plane crashed during the war and he was gravely injured. He couldn't fly anymore and was transferred to a desk job at the British Embassy in Washington DC.

He quickly charmed his way into high society in DC and became so popular that the British Intelligence asked him to spy for them and promote Britain's interests in the USA. Dahl managed to gain support for Britain and even passed valuable stolen documents to the British government. It was also in DC that he discovered his passion for writing while creating propaganda material for American newspapers!

As a schoolboy, Roald Dahl was a taste-tester for Cadbury's chocolate. This may have been the later inspiration for *Charlie and the Chocolate Factory*.

304 Harper Lee only wrote two novels.

Harper Lee's masterpiece *To Kill a Mockingbird* was published in 1960 and gained immediate success, winning the Pulitzer Prize and remaining on the best-selling list for 88 weeks. The book is considered to be a modern classic and is one of the best American novels of all time. The story deals with the racial inequality that Harper Lee observed in her hometown.

Lee was interested in literature ever since she was in school. After graduating, she found an agent. Having written many long stories, he gave her a year's wages and told her to write whatever she wished. A year later, she showed him a rough manuscript, which still resembled a string of long stories more than a novel. Finally, two and a half years later, the book was published. It was an immediate commercial success. However, Harper Lee wrote nothing after the publication of this book until 2015, when she released a novel called *Go Set a Watchman*.

Lee is a private person, so no one knows why she took a long break between her novels. Some say that the success overwhelmed her while others speculate that she had just one story to tell and it was already told in her first book.

In 2007, Harper Lee was awarded the Presidential Medal of Freedom of USA for her contribution to literature.

305 Before writing *The da Vinci Code*, Dan Brown was a pop singer.

Dan Brown is one of the most well-known authors of this generation. His books, *The da Vinci Code* and *Angel and Demons*, are now critically acclaimed films as well. But much before he turned to writing as a career, he was a singer-songwriter! After graduating, he dabbled in a career in music, producing a children's cassette titled *Synth Animals* featuring songs like *Happy Frogs* and *Suzuki Elephants*. He then moved to Hollywood and released an album, *Dan Brown*, in 1993 and another, also titled *Angels and Demons*, in 1994. He started working on his first book, *Digital Fortress*, in 1993 and finally quit to become a full-time writer in 1996.

306 For J. R. R. Tolkien, writing was a hobby, not a profession.

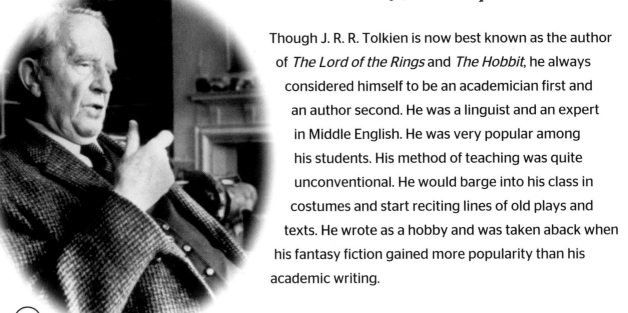

Though J. R. R. Tolkien is now best known as the author of *The Lord of the Rings* and *The Hobbit*, he always considered himself to be an academician first and an author second. He was a linguist and an expert in Middle English. He was very popular among his students. His method of teaching was quite unconventional. He would barge into his class in costumes and start reciting lines of old plays and texts. He wrote as a hobby and was taken aback when his fantasy fiction gained more popularity than his academic writing.

307 George Bernard Shaw never went to school, but won a Nobel Prize and an Oscar.

George Bernard Shaw, an Irish playwright, novelist, essayist and journalist, is best known for his play, *Pygmalion*, which went on to become a successful Broadway musical and Hollywood film, *My Fair Lady*. He is also known for his wit and humour. What he's less known for is the Nobel Prize he won! He is the only person to ever win both a Nobel Prize as well as an Oscar.

He had a difficult childhood and started working at the age of 16. He was largely self-taught. He wanted to be a writer from the beginning of his career and wrote five unsuccessful novels over the next seven years. He eventually found more success as a journalist. He was an active socialist and advocated women's rights. He won a Nobel Prize in literature in 1925 for his play, *Pygmalion*, and an Oscar later for the film of the same name.

George Bernard Shaw was reluctant to accept the Nobel Prize at first because he did not care for public honours, but accepted it at his wife's request as a tribute to Ireland.

308 Rudyard Kipling was the youngest recipient of the Nobel Prize for literature.

Rudyard Kipling was an author who was best known for writing *The Jungle Book*. It earned him a Nobel Prize in literature in 1907, when he was just 42, making him the youngest person to win the prize in that category till date. He was offered the British knighthood on several occasions, but denied them all. He was born in India and though he wrote children's fiction, his stories explored the social and political implications of the British rule in India.

309 Leonid Hurwicz was the oldest person to receive a Nobel Prize.

Leonid Hurwicz was an American mathematician and economist. He came up with the concept of incentive compatibility and mechanism design. He was born in Moscow, Russia, on August 21, 1917. Hurwicz did not begin his formal education until he was nine years old! However, he went on to receive the Sveriges Riksbank Prize in Economic Sciences in 2007 along with Eric S. Maskin and Roger B. Myerson for his contributions to mechanism design theory. Hurwicz was 90 years old when he received the prize!

310 Aladdin wasn't originally part of the Arabian Nights.

The Arabian Nights is a collection of stories that originated in Persia and India in the 8th century. The legend goes that a Persian Sultan, Shahriyar, was once very angry with his wife. So, he ordered her to be killed. After that, he would marry a new woman every day and have her beheaded on the next day.

Eventually, he married a bright, young woman named Scheherezade. At night, she started telling the Sultan a story, but stopped at a very interesting point, saying that it was nearly dawn and she was tired. The Sultan, eager to know what would happen next in the story, decided to spare her life for one night. The next night, she did the same thing. This continued for the next 1,000 nights, by which time the Sultan had fallen in love with her and decided to spare her life. This collection of stories is often called *Arabian Nights*. *Aladdin* is a story often associated with this large volume of stories, but was actually added almost 100 years later by a French translator.

Sindbad the Sailor and *Ali Baba and the Forty Thieves* are two more famous stories that were actually added later on.

311 *Moby Dick* didn't sell its first 3,000 copies.

Moby Dick is Herman Melville's sixth novel. It is the story of Captain Ahab's voyage in pursuit of Moby Dick, a large white whale. It received mixed reviews when it was released and failed to sell even the first 3,000 copies. Today, it is considered to be one of the greatest American novels. Melville's next book, *Pierre*, wasn't received well either. This book was about an author who wrote a book that was badly received, reflecting his bitter feelings about the reception of Moby Dick.

312 There's a novel that doesn't contain the letter "e".

"E" is the most common letter in the English language. It's tough enough to write a sentence that does not contain the letter, let alone an entire novel. But Ernest Vincent Wright was up for the challenge. He worked on a manuscript for years before finally releasing the book, *Gadsby: A Story of Over 50,000 Words Without Using the Letter "E"* in 1939.

It was a self-published book and not well-received in his time. But it was a very ambitious attempt and this book has become a collector's item because of its scarcity.

313 Stan Lee of Marvel Comics used alliterative names so they'd be easier to remember.

Stan Lee is a comic book writer, editor, publisher, actor, voice artist and media producer who is famous for creating many characters for Marvel Comics, including Spider-Man, the Hulk, the Fantastic Four, Iron Man, Thor and the X-Men. He gave all his characters alliterative names, which means that their name and surname began with the same letter. Some of his famous characters include Bruce Banner, Fantastic Four, Pepper Potts, Peter Parker, Green Goblin, Silver Surfer, Sue Storm, Wade Wilson, Scott Summers and many more.

He has actually explained why he uses so many alliterations to name his characters. He says that his memory is terrible, so he figured that if he could remember half of a character's name, the repeated letter would provide a clue for recalling the other half. He also claims that alliterative names and catchphrases are easier for readers to memorise.

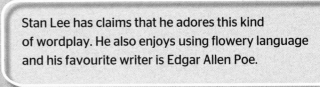

Stan Lee has claims that he adores this kind of wordplay. He also enjoys using flowery language and his favourite writer is Edgar Allen Poe.

314 The most expensive book in the world was bought at $30,802,500.

On 11th November, 1994, Bill Gates bought the original manuscript of *Codex Leicester*, written by Leonardo da Vinci, at Christie's auction house in New York. The manuscript is about 500 years old and is written in da Vinci's own handwriting, accompanied by copious sketches. It covers a wide range of his observations and theories on astronomy, the properties of water, rocks and fossils, and air.

The notebook provides invaluable insight into the life of this great Renaissance mastermind. Leonardo da Vinci was a scientist who was many years ahead of his time. Bill Gates said that he bought the book because he had always been fascinated by da Vinci's ability to work out scientific things on his own and understand things that other scientists in his time didn't. Bill Gates then made the manuscript available online on The British Library website when he launched Windows Vista. You can access it on the following link: http://hammercodex.com/preview1.php

Leonardo wrote all his books in "mirror writing". This means that he wrote in the opposite direction — from right to left — in such a way that it would be readable if looked at in a mirror.

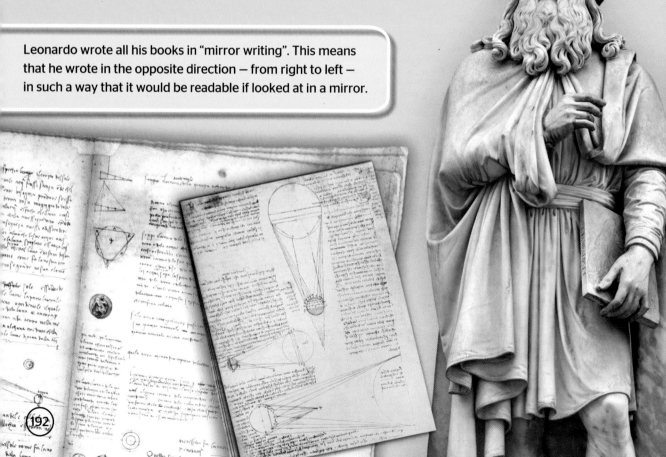

315 There's an unfinished novel called Suspense.

An author named Joseph Conrad started working on a book named *Suspense: A Napoleonic Novel* in 1924. But he died before he could complete the manuscript. The incomplete manuscript has been published after his death. However, the great irony is that the readers will actually remain in suspense about the ending of the book! Conrad was a fairly well-known writer, contributing to the fields of novels, novellas, short stories and essays. He is particularly known for popularising the anti-hero. Interestingly, though he wrote in English, he didn't learn the language till he was in his 20s and always spoke it with a heavy accent.

316 Aristophanes' play, *Assemblywomen*, contains the longest word, containing 171 letters.

The longest word in literature comes from an Ancient Greek play written by Aristophanes. It is the name of a fictitious dish in his comedy, *Assembly-women*. The word is, "Lopadotemachose-lachogaleokranioleipsanodrimhypotrim-matosilphioparaomelitokatakechymeno-kichlepikossyphophattoperisteralektry-onoptekephalliokigklopeleiolagoiosiraio-baphetraganopterygon". The longest word in English literature was coined by James Joyce in *Finnegans Wake*. It is 101 letters long. It is "Bababadalgharaghtakamminarronnkon-nbronntonnerronntuonnthunntrovarrhounawns-kawntoohoohoordenenthurnuk".

ARTY PARTY

Art and art movements are an important part of our cultural history. Some artists, like Leonardo da Vinci, were also great scientists. Others pioneered art movements but were absolutely unknown in their day. Some others were celebrated even as amateur artists. Read on to find out more about art and artists through the ages!

317 Raphael was born and died on the same date.

Raphael was a well-known Italian Renaissance painter and architect. He was born on 6th April, 1483. He also died on 6th April, 1520, at the age of 37. He was the chief architect of the Vatican and designed a number of churches, palaces and mansions. He was a prolific painter. By the end of his life, he had 78 paintings. Along with Leonardo da Vinci and Michelangelo, he forms what is considered as the trinity of Renaissance painters.

318 Vincent Van Gogh sold only one painting in his lifetime.

Today, Vincent Van Gogh is remembered as an eccentric, possibly insane but highly talented painter. He was a prominent painter belonging to an art movement called "impressionism". He was born on 30th March, 1853, in Holland. He had several personal struggles and self-esteem issues, which led to him being labelled as "insane" by many. He remained in Belgium to study art and was determined to give happiness by creating beauty.

Van Gogh then moved to Paris, where he met artists like Pissaro, Monet and Gauguin, who influenced him to paint in the short brushstrokes of the impressionists. After a few years there, he wanted to move to Arles and hoped that his friends would join him there to start a school of art. Gauguin agreed, but the results were disastrous. In a fit of madness, Van Gogh chased him down the street with a razor but ended up cutting off a portion of his own left ear. Eventually, Van Gogh committed suicide in July 1890.

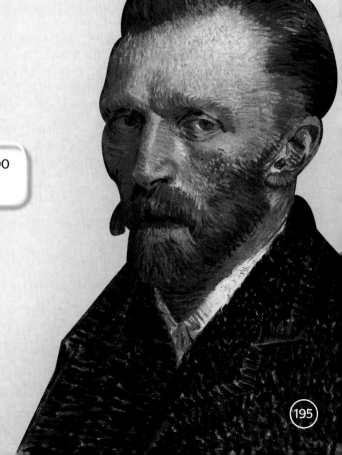

In a short span of 10 years, Van Gogh made almost 900 paintings and 1,100 sketches.

319 Claude Monet's father wanted him to be a grocer.

Claude Monet is one of the most famous painters in the history of art and is a leading figure in the Impressionist movement. In fact, it is said that after an art exhibition in 1874, a critic insultingly described Monet's painting as an "impression", since it was more concerned with light and form than realism. The term stuck and every painting that was painted in a similar style was called an "impressionist" painting.

However, Monet struggled with poverty and depression throughout his life. In fact, his father thought he would make a better grocer than a painter. Even as a student, Monet showed a keen interest towards art. He would fill his notebooks with sketches and caricatures. In fact, he became famous for drawing caricatures of all the people in his town.

Monet was the first painter to paint outdoors. Earlier, painters would paint outdoor scenes from memory. Monet would actually go out and stand in front of the scene he wanted to paint.

320 Titian was the only plague victim to be buried in a church.

Titian was an Italian oil painter born around 1489 in Venice, Italy. Titian grew to be one of the best painters in Venice and had a great influence over Western art. He used clean colours and portrayed an idealistic beauty, both in nature and in people. In the 1530s, he painted a series of portraits for Emperor Charles V. The Emperor was so impressed that he offered a knighthood to Titian! Unfortunately, Titian died of the plague on 27th August, 1576.

The practice in those days was to bury all plague victims in mass graves. But Titian got a special church burial because of his fame and talent.

321 Renoir visited the Louvre to see his own paintings.

Pierre-Auguste Renoir is a well-known French artist. He was born on 25th February, 1841, in France. He showed an interest in art even as a child, when he was working with a porcelain painter. He would go to the Louvre alone to study great paintings and painters. He later joined impressionists like Monet. He gained fame during his lifetime. In 1919, he visited the Louvre to see his paintings hanging amongst the masterpieces of the old masters. He died later that year.

322 Michelangelo wanted to be a sculptor, not a painter.

Michelangelo, born in Italy on 6th March, 1475, is a well-known Renaissance artist. His father didn't encourage his pursuit of art, because it was deemed below the family status. His father wanted him to pursue a career in business. But Michelangelo always wanted to sculpt. He finally studied under Lorenzo de Medici, a retired sculptor.

In 1508, Michelangelo was working on a tomb for the Pope when the Pope insisted that Michelangelo leave that and paint the ceiling of the Sistine chapel instead. Though Michelangelo was reluctant, he agreed and spent the next four years on scaffolding, painting the now famous ceiling.

Michelangelo did not enjoy painting the ceiling at all. He complained that the constant dripping of paint in his eyes was affecting his eyesight. He also once said, "I am not in the right place—I am not a painter."

323 Pablo Picasso's full name had 23 words.

We know Pablo Picasso as one of the most influential modern artists known for pioneering cubism. But he was actually baptised as Pablo Diego José Francisco de Paula Juan Nepomuceno María de los Remedios Cipriano de la Santísima Trinidad Martyr Patricio Clito Ruíz y Picasso. That's quite a mouthful, isn't it? He was named after several saints and relatives.

Picasso was born on 25th October, 1881, in Spain. His father was an art teacher, which sparked Picasso's interest. His father started training him in art from the age of seven. Picasso finished his first painting at the age of 10. When he was 16, he started attending Madrid's Royal Academy of San Fernand. His art attracted the attention of many Parisian art collectors in 1900. Picasso laid the foundation for the cubism art movement. Cubism involves breaking the painting's subject and re-assembling it on the canvas in an abstract composition. He died on 8th April, 1973.

Picasso's first word meant pencil! His first word was "piz", short for "lápiz" the Spanish word for pencil.

324 Edvard Munch received almost no formal training.

Edvard Munch was an expressionist painter. Expressionism was an art movement that aimed to express the artist's inner feelings and emotions instead of reality. *The Scream* is probably the most well-known expressionist painting and the artist who painted it, Edvard Munch, had almost no formal training in the field!

Edvard Munch was born on 12th December, 1863, in Norway. He began a career in engineering, but he gave it up in order to pursue art. He was always a troubled individual because a lot of people who were close to him, like his mother and his sister, passed away when he was just a child. This had a very strong impact on his life.

Munch was interested in drawing from an early age. He was influenced by the Kristina Bohème, a group of writers and artists in Oslo. He started painting in 1881. His early works were extremely intense.

The Scream sold for more than $119 million in 2012, setting a new record at the time.

325 Han van Meegeren made a fortune selling fake paintings.

Han van Meegeren not only forged and sold at least five Vermeer paintings, he also voluntarily confessed his crime. Vermeer is one of the most famous Dutch artists. Han van Meegeren replicated his style so well that even the most experienced art critics thought that these were undiscovered Vermeer paintings. One of his paintings, *Supper at Emmaus*, was hailed by some of the world's most famous art critics as the finest Vermeer they had ever seen. All was going well for Han van Meegeren and he might have got away with his fraud, if it were not for World War II.

During World War II, a forged Vermeer ended up in the possession of Reichsmarschall Hermann Goring, a German. The Dutch were furious that a masterpiece from their national treasure should find its way to the enemy's hands. Han van Meegeren was then charged with treason. In order to save himself from a death sentence, he confessed to forging the painting and selling it. Once it was proved that the painting wasn't an original, he was let off with just a year's sentence.

It is estimated that Han van Meegeren made around $30 million by selling fake paintings.

326 People thought that there was a live model inside Rodin's first sculpture.

Auguste Rodin was a very well-known French sculptor. He was born in a poor family on 12th November, 1840. He wanted to study at the École des Beaux-Arts, but failed the entrance exam thrice. He moulded his first famous sculpture, *The Age of Bronze*, also known as *The Vanquished* in 1876. It looked so realistic that when it was first revealed, people thought he had taken the mould of an actual person! He died on 17th November, 1917, before he could complete his final work — *The Gates of Hell*.

327 Salvadaor Dali was named after his dead brother.

Salvador Dali is a celebrated surrealist artist. He was named after his older brother, who died nine months before he was born. He was born on 11th May, 1904, in Spain. He was kicked out of art school in Madrid! He was greatly influenced by Freud's work on dreams and the subconscious, and a group of surrealists he met in Paris. More emphasis was given to the subconscious than reality during the surrealist movement in art and literature. His paintings feature everyday objects in a dream-like, absurd manner.

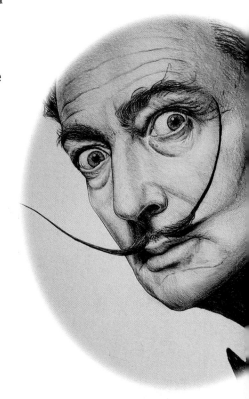

328 Jackson Pollock rarely used a brush to paint.

Jackson Pollock is one of the most famous American painters. He was born on 28th January, 1912. In 1930, he went with his brother to New York to study art. During his first two years in New York, he lived with his brother in relative poverty. He was hired by the WPA Federal Art Project in 1935, after which he started painting commercially.

He is well-known for pioneering an art movement called abstract expressionism. He was one of the first American artists to be considered as a peer of 20th century European masters of Modern Art. He is also known for his unique "drip painting" style. He gained fame and popularity during his lifetime itself. His unique method of painting did not involve the use of a paintbrush. He would let paint drip off knives, sticks or other such objects and then frantically moved around the canvas, trying to find the correct combination of colour, pattern and texture.

While living in New York with his brother, Jackson worked as a janitor at a children's school to make ends meet.

329 Pablo Picasso was considered a suspect in the Mona Lisa theft.

The Mona Lisa was stolen in 1911. The crime was first pinned on a poet, Guillaume Apollinaire, because he had once written that he thought the Louvre should be burned to the ground. Guillaume Apollinaire was a friend of Picasso. After questioning, he tried to pin the crime on his friend! Picasso was then brought in for questioning, but later released. Two years later, it was found that the painting had been stolen by a man named Vincenzo Peruggia, who worked at the Louvre.

Vincenzo Peruggia was an employee at the Louvre, so gaining access to the painting was easy. He hid in a broom closet all day and walked out with the painting under his coat after the museum had shut. He was an Italian patriot who believed that da Vinci's work should be returned to Italy to be displayed at an Italian museum. Peruggia grew impatient and was finally caught when he attempted to sell it to the directors of the Uffizi Gallery in Florence; it was exhibited all over Italy and returned to the Louvre in 1913. Peruggia was hailed for his patriotism in Italy and served six months in prison for the crime.

When Leonardo da Vinci's Mona Lisa was stolen, six replicas were sold as the original, each at a huge price, in the three years before the original was recovered.

330 "Gothic" was originally meant to be an insult.

Gothic art and architecture today is considered to be a classic form of art. However, the term originates from a Germanic tribe called the Goths, who were very barbaric and uncultured. The Goths destroyed the Roman Empire and its classical culture in the 5th century. Critics used the term "gothic" to describe architecture that they found barbaric and uncultured. Today, the term is used to describe art that was characteristic of two great international eras in Europe—from mid 12th century to the 16th century.

331 A painting hung upside-down for 47 days in the Museum of Modern Art.

Henri Matisse, a prominent French artist, painted *Le Bateau* (1953). It was displayed at the Museum of Modern Art in New York on 18th October, 1961. It was hung upside-down for 47 days and was seen by around 1,16,000 people.

Genevieve Habert, a stockbroker, noticed the mistake and notified a guard. Only then was the artwork rehung properly. Other prominent paintings have also been wrongly hung in the past.

332 Willard Wigan once accidentally inhaled his artwork.

Willard Wigan is a "micro-sculptor" whose art is so tiny that it can't even be seen with the naked eye. He began sculpting at the tender age of five! He started making houses for ants because he thought that they needed somewhere to live. He then made them some shoes and hats. That was the humble beginning of his career. His work is so tiny that it sits within the eye of a needle or on a pin head. In order to create such tiny sculptures, Willard enters a meditative state in which his heartbeat is slowed, allowing him to reduce hand tremors and sculpt between pulse beats. Wigan says that he has accidentally inhaled some of his work, one of them being Alice from *Alice in Wonderland*.

333 *Nafea Faa Ipoipo* is the most expensive painting ever bought.

The *Nafea Faa Ipoipo* or *When Will You Marry?* is a painting of two Tahitian women by French artist Paul Gauguin. It was sold for an incredible sum of $300 million in February 2015. It is believed that the buyer hails from Qatar; the identity remains unknown.

Gauguin's paintings portray bright colours and elementary forms, and are often considered as icons of modern art.

334 The Romans made statues with detachable heads.

The Romans specially asked for statues to be made with detachable heads. They did this for a very practical reason. If a hero, ruler or other well-known person lost fame, honour or died, they wouldn't need to commission another whole statue—they could simply make a new head of a more well-known person or new ruler and place it on the old bust! These sculptures had a very typical body with no character and usually wore a toga. Some statues even had detachable hands, limbs or other body parts. But the Romans believed that the identity lay in the head, so most statues had detachable heads.

335 Boys were dressed in blue to ward off evil spirits.

In ancient times, it was believed that certain colours could ward off the evil spirits that lingered over nurseries. Blue was considered to be the colour of the heavens, which is why it was believed that it could ward off evil. As boys were considered to be more precious than girls, they were usually clothed in blue. Although baby girls didn't have any colour associated with them back then, they were usually clothed in black. Only in the Middle Ages did pink come to be associated with girls.

336 The "Mona Lisa" was a spelling mistake.

The Mona Lisa is one of the most famous paintings in the history of art. The reason behind the enigmatic smile on the lady in the painting has been pondered upon by millions of people. *The Mona Lisa* was painted by Leonardo da Vinci between 1503 and 1506. Some even say he continued working on it till 1517!

The painting is thought to be a portrait of Lisa Gherardini, the wife of Francesco del Giocondo. The painting was originally supposed to be named "Monna Lisa". Monna is the short form of "Madonna", which means "My Lady" in Italian.

Today, the painting is considered priceless. In fact, it cannot even be insured! It is kept in the French museum, the Louvre, in a room of its own. It is protected in a climate-controlled environment and encased in bullet proof glass. It cost $7 million to build the room!

In 1956, a man named Ugo Ungaza threw a stone at the painting. This resulted in a small patch of damaged paint next to her left elbow.

337 The word "cartoon" was originally a part of painting terminology.

The word "cartoon" has its roots in the Italian word, "cartone", meaning "pasteboard". That word referred to a full-size preparatory sketch for a fresco, tapestry, mosaic and so on. This large sketch was then placed on the wall, ceiling or whatever surface the final painting was supposed to be on. Tiny pinholes were made in the sketch and dust of the drawing medium (charcoal, graphite, etc.) was rubbed through the holes. Eventually, the entire sketch was transferred! In the 19th century, the term was used to refer to humourous illustrations in magazines and newspapers, and in the early 20th century and onward, it referred to comic strips and animated films.

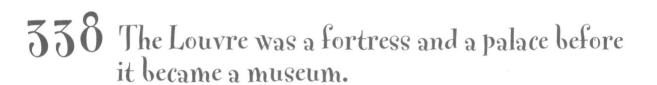

338 The Louvre was a fortress and a palace before it became a museum.

The Louvre is the most famous museum in the world, housing paintings like *The Mona Lisa* and *The Last Supper*. The construction of the fortress began in the Middle Ages by Phillipe Auguste in 1190. In 1364, after the Hundred Years War, Raymond du Temple transformed the fortress into a royal residence for Charles V. It remained the royal residence, increasing in size till 1875. It slowly stopped being the seat of power and was turned into a museum dedicated entirely to culture.

339 There is evidence of paint being used 1,00,000 years ago.

In 2011, South African archeologists found a 1,00,000-year-old reddish-yellow mixture that they feel might have been used as paint by early humans. This paint was an ochre-based mixture. Ochre is a natural pigment found on Earth that varies from yellow to dark brown.

Explorers have also found coloured walls at Dendera in Egypt. They estimate that these walls have been exposed for the last 2,000 years but the colours are still as vivid as they would be if they were freshly painted. It is believed that early humans would mix their paints with a gummy substance, which may be the reason why they are so long-lasting.

340 The world's oldest art is at least 40,000 years old.

Cave art has been discovered in the El Castillo cave in Cantabria, Spain, that is at least 40,800 years old! Cave paintings have been found all over the world. The cave in Spain has several hand stencils that were created by blowing paint over a hand placed against the wall of the cave.

341 Beethoven gave his first public performance when he was just seven years old.

Ludwig van Beethoven is considered by many to be one of the greatest musicians to ever live. He was born around 1770 and was taught music by his father. Even at a young age, it was obvious that he was very talented and his father hoped that he would be a child prodigy. He gave his first performance at the age of seven and a half, at Cologne. He published his first work, "9 variations in C minor for piano" before the age of 12. He soon took over his father as the sole breadwinner in his house and considered his younger brothers to be his responsibility.

In 1801, he confessed to his friends that he thought that he was slowly going deaf. Though he was frustrated to be going deaf as a musician, he did not let his handicap stop him. In fact, he wrote his most famous works after he was completely deaf! He passed away on 26th March, 1827.

Beethoven composed more than 400 pieces of music throughout his life.

342 The Caves of Lascaux are called the Sistine Chapel of prehistoric art.

The Lascaux caves are a set of complex caves in Southwestern France. They contain some of the best-known prehistoric art. This art is estimated to be 17,300 years old. There are nearly 2,000 figures in the cave. More than 900 of these are animals. These animal drawings are consistent with fossils found in the area from that time period. There are paintings of equines, stags, cattle and bison. Strangely, there are no images of reindeer, though that was the main source of food for the artists. Apart from animals, human figures and abstract signs have also been found on the cave walls.

The most famous section of the cave is "The Great Hall of the Bulls". Four black bulls or aurochs are the dominant figures here. One of the bulls is 17 ft long and is the largest animal discovered so far in cave art. Additionally, the artist seems to have captured the bull in motion.

The skill of these ancient artists is evident in one painting called *The Crossed Bison*. The artist has crossed the hind legs of two bisons to create the impression that one bison is closer than the other.

343 Johann Bach was imprisoned for resigning.

Johann Sebastian Bach was a famous German music composer. He was born on 21st March, 1685, into a family of musicians. Though he sang and played several instruments, he is best known for his compositions on the organ. He was a well-known musician even during his time. He was working as an organist for the Duke of Saxeweimar in 1708. In 1717, he was offered a job that would pay him more money. But when he told the Duke about his intention to resign, the Duke got angry and ordered him to be imprisoned for a month. However, Bach used his time constructively and composed a few pieces for the organ while in prison.

344 Ravel's "Bolero" is played somewhere in the world every 15 minutes.

The Bolero is Maurice Ravel's best-known piece of music. It is 15 minutes long and consists of just a single harmony that keeps building up as instruments join in. He wrote it for a friend's ballet in 1928. It is said that it came to him when he was on a holiday. He was tinkling around with the piano when he hit upon a rather insistent tune, which he decided to repeat throughout the piece. Though Ravel considered *The Bolero* to be his least important work, it was always his most popular work.

345 Mozart could write music notes before he could write words.

Mozart is one of the most famous musical prodigies of all time. He composed his first piece of music before he was just five years old! And it took him less than 30 minutes to compose. He was born on 27th January, 1756, in Austria. He began playing and composing music at a very young age and excelled in every genre of music in his time. His parents recognised his musical talents early in life. He was able to pick out chords on the harpsichord by the age of three and he could play short pieces by the age of four. He was taken to play at the Bavarian court when he was just six years old.

He was only 35 when he died, but in that time span, he had already composed more than 600 musical works! He composed 50 symphonies, 25 piano concertos, 12 violin concertos, 27 concert arias, 26 string quartets, 103 minuets, 15 masses and 21 opera works. That's almost one piece of music a day!

When he started playing in public, audiences thought he was a midget because they could not believe that someone so young could actually compose and play so well.

LIGHTS, CAMERA, ACTION!

The illusion of motion has left many spellbound and enraptured. Film has come a long way from the silent black-and-white era of the early 1900s. Though it is one of the newest forms of art, it has a fascinating story to tell. Go on, read all about this magical medium.

346 The first film that told a story was *The Great Train Robbery*.

The Great Train Robbery, produced by Thomas Edison and directed and filmed by Edwin Porter, one of his employees, was the first film that told a story. It is, perhaps, the precursor to the "Western" genre. It is about a train robbery and the chase that follows. It was barely 12 minutes long, but was very popular with the audience. It was also the first film to introduce an editing technique called "crosscutting"—when the film cuts between two scenes taking place at the same time, but in different locations.

347 The first use of special effects was in 1902.

Georges Melies was a French pioneer in the field of film and special effects in the early 1900s. He was actually a magician and his ability to manipulate images earned him the title of a "cinemagician". He was the first person to use hand-painted images in his films and techniques like stop motion, slow motion and dissolve. He discovered the technique of superimposition accidentally when two film strips overlapped each other. He discovered that film needn't show you only what is possible and that is how special effects were born.

He built a studio with elaborate sets, wrote scripts and had actors act them out. His scripts and films like *A Trip to the Moon* and *The Voyage Across the Impossible* often included bizarre voyages and scenes. Scenes like Melies himself juggling his own head or the Sun swallowing people in a spaceship were not uncommon in his movies.

In spite of making so many advances in the field of film-making and pioneering many new techniques, Melies remained unrecognised for most of his life and died a pauper.

348 No one knows who made the first film.

The history of film-making is a long, complex one and there's a lot of dispute over who made the first film. Thomas Edison is credited with inventing the first movie camera and filming a running horse. But this camera was too large and bulky to be taken out of a studio. The Lumiere brothers are credited with inventing the first camera, projector and film.

Auguste and Louis Lumiere's father owned a shop for photographic equipment. Both brothers experimented with the camera and other equipment. They tried to create a camera similar to Edison's, but without its weaknesses. By 1895, they had invented a film camera called the "cinematograph". They filmed workers coming out of their father's factory—the first film. They also filmed a train pulling into the platform.

When the film of the train pulling into the station was screened, audiences ran out of the theatre screaming, as they believed the train would really burst through the screen and run them over!

349 Audiences raved about the performance of an "expressionless" man.

The beginning of the 20th century was a great time to be in film. It was a new medium and people were experimenting with it all over the world. The Soviet government quickly recognised its potential and sponsored many films.

One particularly interesting experiment was carried out by Lev Kuleshov. He was experimenting with editing techniques when he discovered that the audience's reactions to a particular shot changed depending on the shot that was before or after it. He tested this theory practically. In his experiment, he took a shot of a man with no expression and played it before a shot of a coffin. Then, he played the same shot before a shot of a bowl of soup and finally, he played the same shot of the man before a pretty woman lying in a couch. Audiences raved about his performance, talking about how versatile his skill was. They said he looked sadly at the coffin, hungrily at the bowl and with a lot of love at the woman.

The experiment became very famous and this effect came to be known as the "Kuleshov" effect.

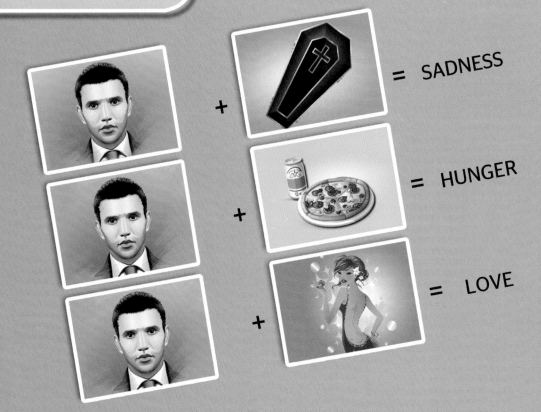

350 The first feature-length film was made in 1915.

The film that set the length for all standard films was a silent film made in 1915, called *The Birth of a Nation*. It was directed by D. W. Griffith. It is considered to be a landmark film in the history of cinema because it used many narrative and cinematographic techniques that had not been used before.

The film follows the story of two households through the civil war and the period in American history just after the war. It has influenced many great directors. The scale of some of the battle scenes are spectacular — considering its era — and remain unmatched even today.

The film was a huge commercial success, but it was criticised for its racial content and portrayal of African Americans as stupid and barbaric. It also portrays the Ku Klux Klan — an extremist organisation that believed in white supremacy — as herric.

Griffith was so affected by the criticism that he made a film called *Intolerance* the next year.

The Birth of a Nation was the first motion picture to be screened at the White House during President Woodrow Wilson's term.

351 Walt Disney was afraid of mice.

Walt Disney, the founder of The Walt Disney Company, famous for his creations, Mickey and Minnie Mouse, was actually petrified of the rodents! Before the famous company was established, Walt had started a company called Laugh-O-Grams when he was 21. But the company didn't do too well and went bankrupt in a short while. He then travelled to Hollywood with just $20 and one suitcase. He eventually ended up creating the most successful cartoon characters of all time. Another little known fact was that he himself lent his voice to Mickey in the first cartoon.

352 Marilyn Monroe might have been born with six toes.

Marilyn Monroe is often called the "sexiest woman" in the world. She was born on 1st June, 1926. A glamourous icon throughout the 1950s, she spent much of her childhood in foster homes. She started her career as a model and went on to become one of the biggest stars of her era.

In 1946, a photographer published photographs of her early modelling career, where it seems that she had six toes. While some say that she had the toe surgically removed, others say it was just a shadow and some sand in the picture. No one knows for sure.

353 The first film with dialogues and sound was The Jazz Singer.

The Jazz Singer (1927) was the first feature-length film with dialogue to be released. These early sound films were called "talkies". Before this, films were "silent". They were usually accompanied by music in the form of a live orchestra in the theatre or were synchronised with musical scores that were played on amplified record players. In the 1920s, technological advances meant that an audio track could be placed in the film itself!

The transition from sound to talkies was not very smooth! Well-known silent film actors in Hollywood found themselves without work due to their thick accents. Many were also rejected for their "voice pitch" being incorrect. Besides, the early sound equipment was very rudimentary, making outdoor shooting nearly impossible. All films had to be shot in studios, limiting many directors. Actors had to constrict their movements as the large, heavy mikes had to be hidden from the camera. Only Charlie Chaplin was making silent films by the end of 1929.

Not everyone believed in the future of "talkies". Harry Warner (one of the founders of Warner Bros.), once said, "Who would want to hear actors talk?"

354 Steven Spielberg is never on set for the last scene in any of his movies.

The production team of *Jaws* faced a lot of problems. They went over-schedule and over-budget because the mechanical sharks kept breaking down. Finally, Spielberg decided not to actually show the sharks on film, but just use music to warn the audience about the arrival of the shark. When the last scene for Jaws was shot, Spielberg was nowhere to be found.

He thought that the crew would throw him into the water when the scene was over since he was such a hard task master. Since then, it became a tradition for Spielberg not to show up for the very final shot for all his films.

355 Fire engines were called by locals during the filming of a scene.

Gone with the Wind, an iconic film by Victor Fleming in 1939, was one of the biggest films of its time. It was the first film to receive more than five Oscars.
One of the most iconic scenes of the film is the burning of Atlanta. This was the first thing to be shot, since it would be the most expensive scene—it cost $25,000.
The scene was shot before the casting was even complete! Stunt doubles were used for lead characters. They burned the studio's back lot, using old sets from other movies. The blaze was so big that frantic locals called the fire department!

356 One of the James Bond actors had never acted before.

James Bond is a series of movies about a suave spy by the titular name who busts the bad guys and gets out of tough situations. Most actors who play James Bond are well established. However, George Lazenby, an Australian man, had never acted before he landed the prestigious role in *On Her Majesty's Secret Service*!

Lazenby first dreamed of playing Bond after watching the film, *Dr. No.* He got his hair cut at Sean Connery's (the actor then playing *James Bond*) barber, bought one of Connery's old suits, got a Rolex and snuck past the secretary into the auditions. In the room, he proceeded to tell all the producers that he had acted all over the world—including Hong Kong and Germany. Only when he met the director did Lazenby admit that he had no idea what he was doing. But they were all so impressed with him that they offered him the lead role anyway.

On Her Majesty's Secret Service was George Lazenby's only role in a film. After this, he only acted in TV commercials, TV series and James Bond spoofs.

357 Harrison Ford was reading lines as a replacement for the lead actor when he got signed on to *Star Wars*.

Harrison Ford was a struggling actor who was finding it difficult to get good roles. Tired of his failure, he gave up acting and became a self-taught professional carpenter to support his wife and children.

In 1978, he was fitting a door at a studio when an executive, who was testing actresses for a new film, asked him to help out by reading the lines written for the male lead, who was absent. Eventually, the director, George Lucas, liked his performance so much that he decided to cast Ford as Han Solo in the film that became one of the world's biggest hits — *Star Wars*.

358 George Lucas quit the Director's Guild to retain his opening credits.

Star Wars is one of the most famous film franchises of all time. One of Star Wars' most well-known attributes is its opening sequence. The movie starts off with a shot of a starry night and the film's theme song starts to play. Yellow credits then start rolling out from the bottom of the screen. They start out large and then shrink as they disappear into the night sky.

Such credits had never been done before and Lucas had trouble getting permission to use them. He had to pay a fine and resign from the Director's Guild to retain these credits.

359 *Ben-Hur* held the record for the maximum Oscars for 37 years.

Ben-Hur is a 1959 American epic historical drama film, directed by William Wyler. It won 11 Oscars, including Best Picture. This was a record that stood till 1997, when *Titanic* also won 11 Oscars and then again in 2003, when *Lord of the Rings: The Return of the King* won 11 Oscars.

Ben-Hur is an adaptation of the 1925 silent film of the same name, which was adapted from Lew Wallace's 1880 novel. The film, set in the 1st century, explores the relationship of two friends practicing different religions.

360 The record for the longest time gap between a film and its sequel is over 63 years.

Bambi was a Disney production made in 1942 and it captured the hearts of audiences all over the world. The film is enjoyed by children even today. The movie tells the adventures of a young fawn named Bambi.

However, Disney didn't create a sequel for *Bambi* until February 2006. *Bambi II* was a direct-to-video offering from Disney and wasn't released in theatre halls. It wasn't exactly a sequel because it covered specific events in Bambi's life, from the time he met his father to the time he came of age in the forest. *Bambi II* was released 63 years and 178 days after the original movie, making it the longest time gap between a film and its sequel.

361 James Cameron drew all the sketches in *The Titanic.*

The Titanic is one of the biggest box office hits of all time and an unforgettable experience for everyone who worked on it. It was directed by James Cameron in 1997 and starred Leonardo DiCaprio and Kate Winslet as the leading actors. It won a record breaking 11 Oscars, including Best Picture and Best Director! It was the first movie in the history of cinema to break the billion dollar mark and gross a total of $1.8 billion.

The film is a fictionalised account of the RMS Titanic that sank in April 1912. In the film, the two main characters, Rose and Jack, fall in love. One of the most iconic scenes in the film is one where Jack is drawing a sketch of Rose. The hands that were shown sketching the portrait belonged to James Cameron. In reality, the sketches were drawn by Cameron. In fact, he drew all the sketches in the leather binder that Jack carries around in the film.

A 64 million l tank was built for the sinking scenes in *The Titanic*. It is the largest shooting tank in the world.

362 David Seidler waited 20 years to make a movie.

David Seidler was always inspired by King George VI because they both shared a childhood difficulty—a stammer. Seidler would listen to the king's radio speeches during the World War and found them very reassuring. He took inspiration from the king, who had learned how to overcome his stammer. When he started researching the monarch, he found out about Logue, a teacher who had helped him overcome his difficulty. One of Logue's sons had his diaries, but to use any of the material he found in them, David would have to obtain permission from the Royal family.

So, David wrote a letter to the Queen mother in 1982, who said that he could use the material after her death since the memories of her dear husband were too fresh and painful. David agreed to shelve the project till the Queen's demise.

The Queen lived to a ripe old age of 101 and finally passed away in 2002. Seidler picked up on his project and finally wrote the film, *The King's Speech*, in 2010.

The film was a huge success, critically and commercially. It was nominated for 12 Oscars that year and won four.

363 The largest film industry in the world is the Indian film industry.

"Bollywood" is the term that is used to refer to the most popular film industry in India, the Hindi film industry. It is a mixture of the words "Bombay" and "Hollywood". India is a multi-lingual country and produces films in many different languages. It is estimated that India produces a total of about 1,000 films a year, of which only 20% is Bollywood. The rest is regional cinema. In contrast, Hollywood produces only half this number!

What's most interesting is that even though India has the largest number of films made per year and the largest ticket sales in the world, it ranks fifth on the list of box office earnings. This is because Indian film tickets are comparatively cheaper than those in other parts of the world.

The history of Indian cinema is rich and dates all the way back to 1896, when a screening of the Lumier brothers' film was held in Mumbai. Indian entrepreneurs ordered the camera and started filming and screening their own films.

The first Indian feature film was made in 1913. It was called *Raja Harishchandra* and was directed by Dadasaheb Phalke.

364 Marlon Brando stuffed his cheeks with cotton balls while auditioning for *The Godfather*.

The Godfather is an iconic 1972 American crime film based on a novel of the same name. The film follows the story and relationship of a fictitious crime family in New York. The film is very prominent in pop culture, with many of its dialogues acquiring a cult status. In the film, Marlon Brando has done a brilliant job of portraying ruthless Mafia leader Don Corleone.
But for his auditions, he stuffed his cheeks with cotton wool! He said that he wanted the Don to look like a bulldog. He also had a very high-pitched voice and said that the cotton wool made him sound more authentic.

365 Disney fired Tim Burton for making a film and then produced that film years later!

Frankenweenie was a short film directed by Tim Burton in 1984. At the time, Burton was a Disney employee. The film is a spoof and homage to the 1931 film *Frankenstein*, which was based on the Mary Shelley novel with the same name. It was the last film that Tim Burton took part in with the Disney staff. He was fired over the film and accused of wasting company resources. They felt the film was too scary for children. So Disney did not release the film and shelved it. But after Burton had success with other films like *Beetlejuice* and *Batman*, the film was released straight to video in 1984. Burton made a feature-length remake of Frankenweenie in 2012.

OTHER TITLES IN THIS SERIES

ISBN 978-93-83202-81-2

ISBN 978-93-84625-92-4

ISBN 978-81-87107-58-3

ISBN 978-93-52760-49-7

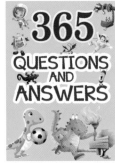
ISBN 978-93-80070-79-7

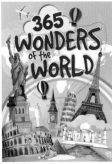
ISBN 978-93-80069-35-7

ISBN 978-93-80069-36-4

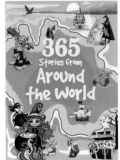
ISBN 978-93-81607-49-7

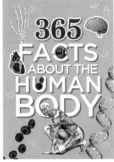
ISBN 978-93-84625-93-1

ISBN 978-93-84225-31-5

ISBN 978-93-80070-83-4

ISBN 978-93-80070-84-1

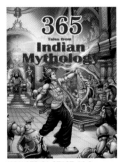
ISBN 978-81-87107-46-0

ISBN 978-81-87107-55-2

ISBN 978-81-87107-56-9

ISBN 978-81-87107-57-6

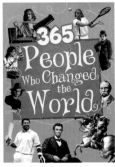
ISBN 978-93-84225-34-6

ISBN 978-93-84225-32-2

ISBN 978-81-87107-53-8

ISBN 978-93-85031-29-8

ISBN 978-93-52764-06-8